"The notion that science and spirituality are somehow mutually exclusive does a disservice to both."

Carl Sagan

Published by:
Viale Industria Pubblicazioni
Torino, Italy – A.D. 2018
viplibri@libero.it

In Deposito Legale presso SBN

ISBN: 978-0-9987098-1-9

*Dedicated to the fine Italian gentleman who
conceived of and published this book,*

Renato Aldo Lorenzo Maria Floris

Actor, Director, Cinematographer, Publisher,
Philosopher, Scholar, Husband

1. Natacha Rambova gazing into a crystal ball.

"...Many smile at what I am writing now, give it no credence, discard it as the phantasms of my brain. But a few years ago these same people would have smiled with equal skepticism at the messages the radio brings us today. How, they would ask, could voices, picked out of the air, be transmitted by an unseen force over miles of empty space? Today no one doubts the validity of radio transmission. It is just another scientific phenomenon to which yesterday we were blind."

Natacha Rambova - *Rudy, An Intimate Portrait of Rudolph Valentino by His Wife, Natacha Rambova*

Table of Contents

The Story-

1   *Exordium*   The Death of Claude Falls Wright

4   *Chapter 1*   The Ousting

12   *Chapter 2*   Love of Her Life

17   *Chapter 3*   Black Carpeting

24   *Chapter 4*   A Trance Meeting

31   *Chapter 5*   The Dead Russian Woman

37   *Chapter 6*   Its Elemental

42   *Chapter 7*   Destination Mystère en Côte D'Azur

50   *Chapter 8*   The Extraordinary Test

54   *Chapter 9*   Rudolph Valentino Intime

61   Rudolph Valentino's "Revelations"

111   And Then

151   The Album

211   Having Their Say

237   The Appendices & Index

The

Story

Exordium

The Death of Claude Falls Wright

Pearl Lagoon, Nicaragua - March 1926.

Rain pelts the muddy grave, sending rivulets onto the mourner's sodden shoes. A matronly woman and two safari-outfitted men stand graveside under a single umbrella, drenched around their edges. Before them, a Pearl Lagoon fisherman fidgets with his straw hat-in-hand. Unfazed by his torrential baptism, he eulogizes.

"Señor Wright. It was no good what happened to him, Señora Eleanor. ¡ Que Dios le bendiga, Señor Wright! "

Eleanor Broenniman weeps with the rain; her sobs not going unnoticed. Her son Edgar and deep-trance medium George Wehner stand by consoling.

"How dismal an end for Claude," whispers Edgar as a gust of wind threatens the umbrella.

"Oh, Edgar! Enough! You're making it worse," shushes Eleanor.

How she suffers; the scenario far surpassing all limits of her withstanding. Remaining steadfast despite, she summons every resolve to honor the final resting place of her dear friend.

Eleanor Broenniman arrived in Pearl Lagoon with Edgar and George Wehner earlier that day aboard a banana freighter from New Orleans. The Pearl Lagoon locals greeted them by jostling to be first to tell them about the dire state of affairs on the Broenniman plantation, located a few hours north along the Wawashang River. They also shared the news of Claude Wright's death, several times and in sorry detail. Despite some discrepancies in the grisly tale, one detail was consistent. The torso of the American gentleman's body washed up on Pearl Lagoon's river bank.

1

The discovery of his remains came as little surprise to the citizens of Pearl Lagoon. Reports of the volatile situation on the Broenniman plantation reached them long before Claude Falls Wright ever arrived. The townsfolk warned him not to adventure north along the Wawashang alone; advice he should never have ignored.

Before embarking on his fatal trek, Claude Wright spent a week in Pearl Lagoon organizing his expedition to the plantation of his fellow Manhattan Theosophist, Eleanor Ray Broenniman. As a member of the Executive Committee of the Theosophic Society of America, Claude accepted the mission enthusiastically on Eleanor's behalf. He would not live long enough to file a single report from the Nicaraguan jungle. If the crocodiles had not left his remnant, there would have been no explanation for his disappearance.

"My, poor, poor Claude," Eleanor weeps on graveside as Edgar continues his hand patting. George struggles with the umbrella as the effort makes him feel faint; his vision blurs. The relentless rain sparks a moment of trance for George and he surrenders to the gathering ethers. In that discarnate moment, he hears Claude Wright's death throes and the thrashing of those crocodiles devouring their meal.

George gazes into the mists to see trails of vapor writhing up from Claude Wright's grave as serpentine apparitions. In an instant, they slither away over the muddy field like tongues with something desperate to say.

"Are you alright, George?" Edgar asks.

George inhales a long breath to return to consciousness, "Now, Edgar, I am, yes."

Over the next few days, Eleanor Broennimen ensured Claude Wright's grave receive its dignified commemoration. She also met with Pearl Lagoon notables to establish a memorial foundation in his name which could be used to benefit children. Eleanor stayed on in Pearl Lagoon for two more weeks while Edgar and George traveled through the jungle by horseback to resolve the labor problems on her plantation.

George Wehner never met Claude Falls Wright and embarked on this journey only as an interlude of psychic service executed within his professional capacity as a deep-trance medium.

The details of Claude Wright's death, the trek by horseback with Edgar along the Wawashang River; George knew precisely how it would transpire because he predicted it all a few months prior in a séance in Manhattan.

Claude Falls Wright's demise was not the only death George predicted that year. Within a month of his return from Nicaragua, he would travel half-way around the world in the opposite direction to the French Riviera where he would prophesize the death of silent film icon Rudolph Valentino.

Chapter One

The Ousting

Seven months earlier in August of 1925, on an eastbound train crossing the American prairies.

The morning panorama is lost on Natacha Rambova, Mrs. Rudolph Valentino. If she does cast a glance, the American heartland streaking past the train's window appears as blurry background to her deep-in-thought. She is still arguing with her husband Rudy, who was by then more than one thousand miles behind her in Hollywood.

Natacha scowls at the white-linened table before her; spread with an array of fragrant pastries, a small pot of tea, her ivory cigarette holder and matching case. She has been up since dawn and long before her travel companions, her Aunt Teresa and Rudy's business manager, George Ullman.

The train rattles across a trestle, issuing a long whistle as it speeds over the river below. The August air is stifling and prompts Natacha to crank the window lower. Despite her refined surrounds, she is not admiring any vista. She is tormented by words, words and more words she wished she'd said before leaving Los Angeles, vexed by regret and still determined to have her say.

She glances at her wristwatch with its thinly-cut moonstone dial sparkling in diamond adornment; a Christmas gift from Rudy a few years earlier.[1] Not so long ago those diamonds would have inspired love for her husband. Today she whispers, "I'm buying a new watch!"

Natacha opens her cigarette case, makes a selection and presses it into the cigarette holder; strike and light. The smoke wakes Aunt Teresa who stirs in a curtained compartment nearby.

She yawns as she arrives to sit down across from Natacha, "How long have you been awake, dear?"

"For hours." her niece answers.

"Well, go back to bed. Read something to take your mind off things."

Natacha stands to take her Aunt's advice as George Ullman enters the car.

He appears exhausted, despite a night's rest. Staging Natacha's departure from Los Angeles meant long hours for him throughout the past week. His tough work week was further exacerbated by Rudy's ill temper. The dissolution of his marriage to the woman he still clearly loved, had him in a very bad mood.

George Ullman rubs his eyes and resets his eye glasses, "Good morning, Teresa. Do you have another letter for me to mail at the next station, Natacha?"

"No. I do not." Natacha greets him by wrapping her robe tightly around her waist and snapping, "I won't write him another word." She turns and heads toward her sleeping compartment.

Aunt Teresa waits a moment before saying to George Ullman,

"When we get to Manhattan, you must find her representation. She can not continue in this state."

"I will. I will," he responds, taking a seat to gaze out the window.

The silence of their breakfast is interrupted only by the noise of the train clacking on across the countryside taking them closer to New York City and a hopeful ceasefire in Rudy and Natacha's bitter domestic warfare.

Natacha kept her word and her final letter to her husband was sent the day before. It was a lengthy letter of frantic confessions, knowing each one would further enrage. Again, she asked Rudy why she was being exiled for a brief liaison with a cameraman, when he entertained beautiful co-stars in his bungalow on the United Artists' studio lot every day. Again, she argued how cruel he was to sign a contract with United Artists denying her a role in his future films. She raged as she wrote that last letter; asking how dare he hire detectives to follow her?

Natacha falls back to sleep that morning, unaware her marriage

5

to America's most swooned-upon matinee idol has effectively destroyed her Hollywood career. Any perspective is obscured by the fresh trauma of their parting. As her last letter wends its way towards Rudy, Natacha dreams of retaliation for such a brutal abuse of her art and soul.

Natacha Rambova met Rudolph Valentino in 1920 when she interviewed him for the lead role in Alla Nazimova's production of *Camille*. As the film's art director, costume and set designer, Natacha approved Rudy's candidacy and he was hired on the spot. She would later recall it was not, for her, love at first sight but Rudy's persistent wooing paid off. She felt an affinity with his loneliness and found his inability to tell a joke to be endearing. Journalist Herb Howe would recall the first time Rudy mentioned Natacha to him.

" Rudie (sic) was lonely. I never knew a lonelier man. He craved affection so.

I remember the first time he spoke Natacha's name to me. We had had dinner in his one room kitchenette apartment in the Formosa. He had engaged a woman to come and serve for the occasion and it was wistfully festive. I had done the first stories about him and he was deeply grateful...

Rudie showed me some of his first notices proudly. While I was waxing fervent over his prospects, he tentatively mentioned the name of Natacha Rambova. Had I heard of her? I hadn't. She was doing some really remarkable sets, he said. He thought her a fine artist...

'She's a wonderful girl, very much alone like myself. I go to her house evenings and we talk about things that interest us, things that don't seem to interest many people here; books, new plays, the modern art movement and of course our work. Our tastes are very similar'..." [2]

It was not long before Natacha returned Rudy's romantic advances and they began living together in a small bungalow on Hollywood's Sunset Boulevard.

Their love affair complicated because Rudy was then still a married man. When he moved into Natacha's cozy bungalow, he and his wife, actress Jean Acker were separated but not divorced.

Despite having no divorce papers in hand, Rudy considered his marriage to Jean, effectively over. She infamously rejected him on their wedding night and they never shared a single bed together. A scorned Rudy moved on from his wedding night rejection to soon enjoy his wild success onscreen. This inspired his wife Jean to delay divorce and instead hire private detectives to spy on her husband as he carried on with his new love and mistress, Natacha Rambova.

When Natacha and Rudy fell in love, she was the bigger star in Hollywood, having worked as a costume and set designer on movies with Cecil B. DeMille and Alla Nazimova. Rudy's first hit feature, *The Four Horsemen of the Apocalypse* had yet to be released. He would not be granted status as a household name until his signature film *The Sheik*, premiered in the fall of 1921.

Rudy and Jean Acker would finally divorce in early 1922. Believing the divorce final, Natacha and Rudy married in Mexicali, Mexico. This marriage was quickly annulled when the Los Angeles County District Attorney brought charges of bigamy against Rudy.

It seemed Rudy's divorce from Jean Acker stipulated he wait one year before remarrying. The fact his marriage to Natacha took place in Mexico did not alter the court's ruling and only served to give the appearance that Rudy and Natacha were attempting to circumvent the law. The court ruled their Mexicali marriage invalid and stipulated they endure a one year separation before remarrying. They would marry again in March of 1923 to live at last as husband and wife.

Throughout this time, Rudy welcomed his wife's artistic input his popular movies and in a spirit of eager collaboration, Natacha assumed the role of her husband's creative adviser. As her influence intensified, Rudy's screen performances were artistically elevated and the quality of his films received emphasis. However, this caused some fans of his fans to grumble and resent her very presence.

In the 1920's, social dictates deemed a wife's place in the home and there primarily in the kitchen. With Natacha's notable absence of apron, iron and frying pan, she was above all perceived as a poor wife for Rudolph Valentino. Although photographs of her exuding a general ennui did not win her a legion of fans, this image belied her behind-the-scenes reality. Those who knew Natacha remember her as a happy woman with an easy laugh. She received high praise for her artistic contributions to her husband's films in trade publications but was nevertheless often the target of theater audiences' disapproval.

Rudy's employers exploited their angst. They believed unrest might remedy one challenge they faced in marketing heart-throb Rudolph Valentino. For the moguls, there was enticing potential in allowing Rudy's fans to believe he was unhappy in his marriage, thereby nurturing their sympathy and dreams of being "his".

Press releases were issued implying he took female fans to his dressing room and throughout the Valentino marriage, the motion picture industry portrayed Natacha as a lovely yet persistent thorn in Rudy's attractive side. Their innuendo cast her as self-serving, aloof and cold while directing all compassion towards Rudy. Natacha would recall,

"...Rudy had pride, a legitimate man's pride and they worked on that. They commenced bringing him clippings which said, 'Mrs. Valentino wears the pants...too bad Rudy can't be his own boss,' and so forth and so forth. These rankled. Eventually if I so much as observed it was a nice day, Rudy, about to agree, would catch himself and say, 'No, its not!' Of course I realized how he felt, he didn't want to be putty even in his wife's hands. We would laugh about the clippings; nevertheless, they made a wedge." [3]

Rudolph Valentino's rise to international stardom over those few short years is in great measure due to his successful collaboration with and artistry of his wife, Natacha. Unfortunately, their partnership would be short-lived. Rudy was a traditional man in regards to the subject of domesticity and as much as he appreciated and respected his wife's artistry, he also wished for her to stay home, bear and rear his children. For Natacha, the pressure of producing Rudy's movies and his offspring loomed large and as a world of women swooned over her husband's every move and openly pined to take her place, her marriage rocked towards a tumultuous end.

Seeking solace and counsel during their troubled times, Rudy and Natacha delved into spiritualism, participating in séances and automatic writing sessions. Natacha believed Rudy possessed psychic ability and she spoke publicly about his growing reliance on two spirit guides; Black Feather, an American Indian dispensed advice about Rudy's daily life and Mesolope, an ancient Egyptian shared direction of a more arcane nature. George Ullman explained,

"...It must not be thought that Valentino was superstitious in any small and trivial way. He had no objection to spilling salt, walking under a ladder, whistling in dressing rooms, beginning a picture on a Friday or sitting down with thirteen at a table. These things he ridiculed.

The psychic never became a religion to him but he yielded to its mesmerism more than to any other form. This was entirely due to the influence of his wife who was a firm believer in the occult and initiated him into its mysteries..." [4]

Rudy was further initiated into the occult mysteries by his friend, screenwriter June Mathis and her mother, Virginia or "Jenny". Both mother and daughter Mathis encouraged Rudy's immersion into spiritualism as they were ardent believers in life-after-death and communication with the deceased. When Jenny died in 1922, she allegedly communicated with her daughter June and with Rudy during one of his automatic writing sessions.

Natacha was so convinced of Rudy's psychic talents, in 1923 she encouraged him to publish a small book of his psychic poetry titled, *Daydreams* with publisher Bernarr MacFadden. Natacha explained to MacFadden how Rudy channeled the poems as they were transmitted to him from famous deceased poets via his two spirit guides, Black Feather and Mesolope. She went on to explain how the mysterious initials opening each poem revealed the identity of the famous author transmitting from beyond.

"Natacha called attention to the true authorship of 'The Gift-Book' (James Whitcomb Riley); 'The Love Child' (Lord Byron); 'Gypsies' (Robert Browning); 'At Sunrise Tomorrow' (Elizabeth Barret Browning); and Rudy's favorite, 'Glorification' had actually come from the astral pen of that good gray poet Walt Whitman." [5]

Bernarr MacFadden published *Daydreams* which became an immediate best-seller. [6]

Throughout 1923-1924, séances, automatic writing sessions and heeding the advice of deceased spirit guides became Rudy and Natacha's daily de rigueur.

"...Under intense harassment by his fans and the press, Rudy

9

found welcome solace in any altered state that allowed him to feel safe from outside intrusion... As he became more proficient at slipping in and out of a trance and writing lengthy directives from his master guides while in a state of semi-consciousness, the barrier between his troubled earthly world and his peaceful astral plane grew thinner. " [7]

Storm clouds first threatened the Valentino's marriage during the filming of his movie *Monsieur Beaucaire* in 1924. As the movie's art director, Natacha oversaw many aspects of the lavish production and her demands decimated the film's budget several times. This sparked frequent arguments between Rudy and Natacha.

When *Monsieur Beaucaire* premiered, many fans attributed Rudy's overall lack of action to Natacha's influence. Although *Monsieur Beaucaire* would be heralded as her artistic masterpiece, the future of Rudy and Natacha's artistic collaboration seemed doomed from then on. He would subsequently sign a contract with United Artists eliminating her from any role in the production of his films. She reacted furiously and considered the contract the fatal blow to their marriage.

In a gesture of appeasement, Rudy and George Ullman agreed to fund and produce a movie she would write and produce titled, *What Price Beauty*. The movie was based on the lengths to which women go in search of beauty and a man's dilemma in choosing between the love of a simple woman and the appeal of a glamorous bombshell. George Ullman implored Natacha to first secure a contract securing distribution or run the risk of having no audience for her film.[8] Proceeding despite his caveat, *What Price Beauty* went into full production in the spring of 1925.

Meanwhile Rudy and Natacha's arguments grew louder and longer and their home often tense and silent in the aftermaths. As Natacha's mother Winifred Hudnut, "Muzzie", would recall,

"...It seemed rather hopeless for us to smooth over the difficulties between these over-tired and temperamental children. They were both too proud, too hasty and impetuous..." [9]

Throughout the summer, Rudy spent most of his time in his United Artists' bungalow and Natacha most evenings away from home working on *What Price Beauty* in her own beach bungalow she leased as hideaway.[10] In a pique of paranoia, Rudy hired private detectives to follow her and capture any evidence of infidelity. The first report from the detectives informed him Natacha spent an afternoon alone with *What Price Beauty's* married cameraman, D. J. Jennings.[11]

When confronted, Natacha denied infidelity and was outraged over Rudy's invasion of her privacy. This instigated a final showdown between Mr. and Mrs. Valentino which resulted in their dramatic separation.

Rudy asked George Ullman to establish a new production company to serve as his corporate alter ego, one which would eliminate Natacha from any future role in his business. When informed of Rudy's demands, Natacha did not hesitate to sign on every dotted line.

On the day of their scheduled parting, Natacha met with George Ullman to sign away her business partnership with Rudy. They then all motored to the train station to convince the press they were merely embarking on an amicable "marital vacation."

Headlines blared news of the Valentino's separation and speculation was rife. It was widely reported Rudy instigated the split because Natacha refused to bear his children. He did not discourage the rumor when he told the press,

"...There is no plan on my part at this time to consider a marriage to anyone else. The time will come probably but it is far off. When that time comes, I shall choose to have a wife whose tastes are thoroughly domestic and who is inclined to have children. "[12]

Rudy and Natacha said their good-bye in a display of nervous giggling for the benefit of gathered press and newsreel cameras. Despite the fanfare, she was furious and could not leave Los Angeles fast enough and Rudy seethed believing he was the "cornuto", the betrayed. As Natacha leaned down for a last kiss, no one present that day realized this would be their last kiss and the last time they would ever see each other.

Chapter Two

The Love of Her Life

Manhattan, August 1925.

By the time Natacha, Aunt Teresa and George Ullman arrived in New York City, it was impossible for them to avoid the press or their reports. News boys waved their papers high as they yelled the tale of the Sheik's separation. Magazine stand owners stacked their fresh copies and the *New York Evening Graphic's* boot jacks bellowed the news up and down Broadway. In nearly every article, Natacha was portrayed as the difficult wife who refused to bear Rudy's children. [13]

As much as Natacha outwardly comported herself as a dignified estranged wife, inwardly she was already on her defense. On August 24, she summoned press, stood before a table strewn with letters from Rudy and announced she was about to write a tell-all book about her failed marriage. Ridiculous captions spread word of her plan with one claiming she left "The Sheik" because she was sick and tired of eating spaghetti. [14]

Anticipating the scandalous exposé, reporters badgered Natacha with questions about Rudy's public appearances in Los Angeles with his Hungarian co-star Vilma Banky on his arm and his citation for speeding with a charge of driving under the influence. For Aunt Teresa and George Ullman, Natacha's distress with the coping was painful to witness. George Ullman would recall one exchange with her shortly after their arrival in New York.

"...I do not mean to imply that Natacha had definitely given up all hope of reconciliation. For I recall one morning when I went out to see her, about ten o'clock, she appeared in a white negligee gorgeously embroidered in gold, with her luxuriant hair braided in two long loose braids down her back, her face pale, her eyes delicately ringed from a sleepless night and her whole attitude one of wan dejection.

I was determined to question her definitively to see if I could find out what she really thought and what she proposed to do.

'Do you really love Rudy?' I asked.

Twisting her hands together, in a small voice she replied,

'I...I don't know!'

'Do you want to go back to him?'

'I...I don't know!'

'Do you want to get a divorce and lose Rudy out of your life forever?'

She paused at this and stared at me with her great eyes full of woe.

'I...I don't know!' she faltered and then burst into a flood of tears. Whereupon I knew no more than when I began to question her. Nor, am I convinced did she." [15]

Before George Ullman boarded a train home to Los Angeles, he negotiated a contract for Natacha with Harry J. Cohen, former manager of the foreign department of Metro Pictures Corporation. He also negotiated a second contract for her with Daniel Carson Goodman, the head of production at F.B.O. Pictures, (Film Booking Offices of America, Inc.)[16] Daniel Goodman was developing what he felt to be the perfect film vehicle for Natacha; a movie based on a story by Laura Jean Libbey titled, *Do Clothes Make the Woman*. Harry Cohen closed the deal for Natacha's appearance in the movie with J.I. Schnitzer, Vice President in charge of production for F.B.O. Pictures. Filming was scheduled to begin on November fifteenth on the east coast guaranteeing no unpleasant return to Hollywood for Natacha.

Her screen debut as an actress would be in a modernization of Laura Libbey's story with a script adapted by John C. Brownell.[17] *Do Clothes Make the Woman* provided Natacha with an immediate excuse to travel to France, ostensibly to purchase a wardrobe for the film. However, she would sail for France with the intention of filing for a divorce in Paris.

Natacha returned to New York City aboard the *S. S. Leviathan*, which sailed from Cherbourg, France on Election Day, 1925. She arrived with forty trunks of newly purchased clothing for *Do Clothes Make the Woman* and still fuming over her failed marriage. She announced,

"In Paris I did it. I applied for a divorce. Rudy said that when I was ready to cook and keep house, he would take me back. Fancy that. He would like to keep me basking in his reflected glory." [18]

Upon her arrival in Manhattan she learned Rudy was also in the city for the opening of his latest film, *The Eagle*. Although their paths would nearly cross by a few city blocks, neither made the slightest attempt to contact the other.

Filming began on *Do Clothes Make the Woman* within days of her return with the movie being directed by Harry O. Hoyt and British actor, Clive Brook cast to star opposite Natacha. She held every reason to believe this would be her big break into an acting career and told one reporter,

"...My whole life will be devoted to my career. I want to be a successful actress; by that I mean a success in other ways than merely financial. When I come on stage I do not want to be thought of as Mrs. Valentino, wife of the Sheik. I want to be considered as a young woman who is trying desperately to be a success...." [19]

For Natacha, this drive for success as a single woman meant hyper-activity. She not only worked on the F.B.O. set of *Do Clothes Make the Woman,* she engaged in a variety of activities and at a frenetic pace. She told one reporter that fall she was writing a novel and authoring a comprehensive book on costume design; this while designing the wardrobe for an upcoming Broadway show.

She was also delving deeper into the occult and began attending a gathering of like-minded acquaintances who called themselves, the "Bamberger Circle" or the "Saturday Nighters". The group convened in the home of Mrs. Harry Bamberger, a glamorous New York socialite who hosted the circle with the purpose of holding séances and studying all aspects of spiritualism and theosophy or the "Wisdom Religions".

The regular members of Mrs. Bamberger's circle included Natacha, her mother, "Muzzie", three mediums: Alpha Gabriel, a medium and inspirational speaker, Miriam Epstein who specialized in automatic writing and George Wehner, a deep-trance medium. Mrs. Leopold (Mrs. Harry Bamberger's mother) also attended as well as Marian Hauver, the two women referred to as the "Joys", Dr. Jervan, Ernst Strauss, Albert Mulladay, editor of *Aviation* magazine and a stenographer. [20]

The Saturday Nighters acted primarily as séance sitters for the mediums who created the ambiance depending on their individual process and the spirit guides they summoned. Natacha was enthralled by the Saturday Nighter experience and it was not long before she announced she was hosting her own séance.

By December fifteenth, after one month of filming, F.B.O. Pictures announced their seven reel film starring Natacha Rambova was being cut and edited. The announcement also revealed a title change to *When Love Grows Cold* and the star of the film was not billed as Natacha Rambova but, "Mrs. Rudolph Valentino."

The ploy to exploit her newsworthy divorce infuriated Natacha and she protested, fearing the title change implied she was profiting from her divorce. She did not wish to give the impression the film was a true representation of her martial situation. F.B.O. ignored her complaints and proceeded to launch promotional material for the movie in trade journals, specifically marketing the film with tips on how to entice audiences by using the name Mrs. Rudolph Valentino. [21]

"Natacha, of course means nothing, but Mrs. Rudolph Valentino, her name in private life, is 'something-else' again!" [22]

Natacha's final days of retakes on the F.B.O. set were completed under protest and she focused her attention on the planning of her first séance. Throughout filming she confided in her co-star, Clive Brook and director Harry Hoyt, sharing her enthusiasm over those weekly séances at Mrs. Bamberger's. [23] They were consequently not surprised when she invited them to attend the séance she was organizing. Both men initially demurred, but Natacha insisted by arguing they might in the least find the experience educational.

"So you sit in a circle in the dark and commune with the dead?" Clive Brook asked.

"That depends on the medium's spirit guides," Natacha replied.

"Then what I might hear will depend on the spirit guide the medium summons from the other side?"

Natacha explained, "Each medium acts as a vehicle for those spirits but mediums do not choose who will speak through them."

"So if I do accept your invitation, Natacha, who might I expect to hear from during your séance?"

"I don't know, Clive, as I have yet to book a medium. If it is Alpha Gabriel, then you will hear inspirational voices. If I retain Miriam Epstein then you will hear from the Indian spirits she calls her "fun-makers" or perhaps you shall hear from her guide, Freda. If I am able to have George Wehner conduct the séance then you shall hear from the American Indian chief, White Cloud."

"Well, Natacha," Clive blustered, "White Cloud, Freda! You have made me curious. I'll go!"

Chapter Three

Black Carpeting

Manhattan, December 1925.

George Wehner did not trust show business folk and he considered them to be tremendous phonies. It was for this reason he hesitated to respond to a memo left on his desk; Natacha Rambova phoned with a request he conduct a private séance. George thought initially to refuse her invitation, wishing to keep his affiliation with her within the gatherings at Mrs. Bamberger's home on Saturday nights. He changed his mind only after his spirit guide, the American Indian chief White Cloud insisted he do so. George's faith in the spirit voice of White Cloud was implicit and had been his entire life. Consequently, it was only a minimal hesitation before he returned Natacha's call and scheduled a séance.

George Wehner was then a sought-after psychic who catered to those A-list Manhattanites reveling in the trend of occultism. Without a doubt his panache in all things séance had taken him comfortably far in his other-worldly trade. His personal appeal certainly contributed to his success; he was a handsome, slightly-built man, five feet five inches tall,[24] thirty-four years old with a business-like demeanor.[25] Despite his suspicion of celebrity, George was well-received by the well-known.

Within a few days, George finds himself knocking on the front door of Natacha's penthouse apartment at 9 West 81st Street. Any

17

hesitancy he might have felt accepting her invitation vanishes the moment the door swings open.

George is mobbed by a pack of yapping, tiny dogs as a butler takes his hat and coat to turn and make the announcement over the ruckus, "Mr. George Wehner has arrived, Madam Rambova."

Natacha appears to make her memorable impression. She is dressed in a tightly wrapped purple satin floor-length gown and an extravagantly long Persian brocade housecoat of gold and silver lamé which is lined in a brilliant red fabric matching her signature turban.[26]

George works his way through panting pups to greet Natacha and enter a grand room to be immersed in the exotic; black carpeting spreads wall-to-wall creating a plush canvas for the room's eclectic appointment of pale gray walls, silver-painted woodwork and over-sized, modern furniture upholstered in black velvet.

George greets Natacha and her mother Muzzie, who is reclining on one of the black velvet sofas. Muzzie wears a clinging gown of jade green and a diaphanous duster of rose and gold velvet. Extending her bejeweled hand to George as if in some royal gesture, she eyes the quizzically-dressed medium from his western-styled shirt with its pearl buttons to his shiny black cowboy boots.

Natacha introduces the other séance participants, or sitters to George: Clive Brook, Harry O. Hoyt and Natacha's friend and chanteuse, Donna Shinn Russell.

George surveys the room and slips away for one moment. He steps up a wide stair to exit through two high French doors which are draped in yardage of vermilion velvet. Swinging the doors open, he steps out onto a topiary terrace twinkling with the lights of Central Park and the city beyond.

He pauses to turn and observe the movements of those gathered inside; their gestures, choice of clothing and auras. Within a few minutes Natacha beckons for George to join her in the room she's prepared for the séance; a dining room replete with a chandelier crafted in the shape of a morning glory blossom, laced with tendrils spiraling low over the center of the table. George is pleased with the setting, its glittering crystal display and polished lacquer.

"Would this be to your satisfaction?" Natacha asks.

"Oh, Natacha, It's perfect. But the lighting must be precise as you know. Can we dim the chandelier?"

Natacha beckons for the butler, "Yes, George. Certainly."

In New York City in December of 1925, the services of spiritualists adept in a variety of occult activity could be retained to satisfy every price range. It was a precipitous time to be a psychic as the hiring of someone to commune with the dead on your behalf reached the height of popularity. The timing of this phenomena has historically been attributed to the catastrophic loss of life during World War One.

Over eighteen million people died as a result of the global conflict leaving millions more as relatives and loved ones of the fallen. Vulnerable in their grief and desperate to commune with deceased family members, the stricken sought comfort in the presence of mediums and psychics who claimed they could channel the dead. From the more serious mediums such as George Wehner to gypsies camped on a street corner, the "other side" practitioners were making good money as the astral plane became an acceptable and popular destination.

Egyptologist Howard Carter's discovery of the tomb of Tut Ankh Amon in 1922, charged these dabblings in the afterlife with the added intrigue of new mysteries from the land of the pharaohs. The desert sands and all things Egyptian contributed in great measure to the growing acceptance of crystal balls, tarot cards and séances.

The author of the Sherlock Homes crime fiction detective series, Sir Arthur Conan Doyle announced he was a true believer in the occult and openly endorsed spiritualistic efforts. He owned a bookshop in London where he sold occult reading material and founded the Hampshire Society for Psychical Research. For Sir Arthur his psychic research was of world significance as he felt spiritualism to be a New Revolution; one that could bring comfort and peace of mind to people mourning the loss of loved ones.

The Spiritualist movement was not without its adversaries with American magician and self-appointed anti-spiritualist crusader, Harry Houdini advertising his ability to defraud mediums. Of course this provided advertising for his own act of illusory escape tricks. The debate raged between Houdini and Doyle which served to further intensify popular interest.

If you were not someone convinced occult behavior was the devil's handiwork, you were undoubtedly sitting in séances, gazing into a crystal ball or having a fortune teller read your tarot cards in a small tent or a darkened room. The lure of the mysterious gripped

America's imagination with the occult contributing to the roar of the 1920's; as equally as embraced as a flask of bootleg whiskey or a bathtub full of homemade gin.

Occult activities varied according to one's social status with certain practices deemed more respectable than others. The genre of spiritualism embraced by Natacha, Muzzie, Mrs. Bamberger's Saturday Nighters and George Wehner reflected their social status. They alleged to approach the entire subject as students and their involvement to be psychical research. They made it clear they were not merely seeking a sensational result or hair-raising display. By assuming this superior and academic posture they avoided the pitfall of being perceived as common; or worse of being accused of being devil worshiping witches and warlocks.

George's caliber of mediumship allowed him to cater exclusively to Natacha and Muzzie's haute world with his impeccable style contributing to his professional charisma. According to all first-hand reports, he was convincing and graced the homes of his clients with the elegance of a prince; a psychic prince with a penchant for well-tailored suits, western apparel and cowboy accessories.

In Natacha's dining room, preparations for her first séance continue as the butler dims the morning glory chandelier. Natacha, Muzzie, Clive Brook, Harry Hoyt and Donna Russell take their seats around the table. George shares a few instructions before he relaxes into his chair and closes his eyes. With the sitters as witnesses in the darkened room, his head drops back, his mouth agape. His breathing slows as he snores lightly. Natacha and Muzzie are familiar with his process and lead the sitters in reciting the Lord's Prayer in unison.

"Our father who art in heaven, hollowed be thy name..."

George begins to roll his head side to side. He claws feebly at his throat with his right hand and seems to pant. The sitters continue with the incantation,

"Thy kingdom come, thy will be done..."

George startles the gathering by sitting bolt upright and opening his eyes to stare into the room's shadows. He begins whistling a soft wavering melody. After a few minutes his whistling stops and he relaxes again into his chair, eyes closed. To the uninitiated sitters, George appears to have just fallen asleep; Natacha and Muzzie know this signals his spirit's departure from his body.

"In the name of the Father, the son and the holy ghost, Amen."

The booming voice of White Cloud then speaks through George, greeting the sitters one by one. In his broken English he then ushers in other spirits he acknowledges on the astral plane who wait to deliver their messages for the sitters. George does not pause between their messages and segues from one spirit to the next while speaking in a free flowing monologue of changing voices.

In just more than one hour the spirits have all spoken, George draws a deep breath and opens his eyes. This signals the end of the séance.

By the reaction of the sitters, George felt his first séance for Natacha to have been an "extraordinarily fine" one and he was able to transmit meaningful messages for everyone except Muzzie.[27] Natacha wept being so moved by George's performance and insisted he cancel all bookings to hold séances for her alone.

Muzzie would not be disappointed for long as George held a private séance with her the following day. She was astounded by the accuracy of his messages and relieved he had nothing but positive projections for her daughter's future. This was especially reassuring as Muzzie was prepared to sail to France the following day and the uncertainty of Natacha's emotional well-being was foremost in her mind. She was so calmed by George's positive outlook, she surprised him with an invitation to sail with her to France.

She tried to convince him to visit her and her fourth husband, cosmetics tycoon Richard Hudnut at their grand chateau on the French Riviera. She could think of no finer place to channel the dead than high over the harbor at Juan les Pins and the Mediterranean Sea. George would disappoint Muzzie, explaining he had a prior commitment to conduct a series of séances for the American Society for Psychical Research.

Although he was unable to accept Muzzie's offer, George knew well an affiliation with Natacha Rambova, her mother and Richard Hudnut, could be a gold-gilt opportunity for him professionally. He was above all ambitious and cultivated his high society clientele with

21

finesse; finesse and a gift of flawless gab tinged with enough knowledge of the gab's recipient to mystify consistently.

Despite George Wehner's subsequent and dominating presence in Natacha Rambova's life from the fall of 1925 until 1930, he has remained in the shadows of her life story. This occult phase of Natacha's life was no whim and George Wehner no mere footnote. He was a deep-trance medium in which she held complete confidence and trusted as a devoted travel companion. For as fate had it, George Wehner bonded with Natacha when she was at her most vulnerable. Mourning the loss of her love Rudy and bitter over her Hollywood debacle, Natacha embraced the medium's uplifting presence and ethereal consultations.

Despite her abrupt exodus from Hollywood, Natacha still reigned as the icon of high fashion and her divorce from "The Sheik" provided unending fodder for gossip columnists coast to coast. Contributing to the furor, the producers of *When Love Grows Cold* timed their movie's release with precision by premiering the film just as news of the Valentino's divorce became headlines. With the added interest of Rudy's new block-buster film, *The Eagle* opening in theaters, he and Natacha owned the headlines.

Unfortunately for Natacha, most of the reams of news reportage continued to be hostile towards her and she grew distressed as she was called "everything from Messalina to a dope-fiend."[28] When asked if she was affected by the name-calling she replied,

"I was tortured. I was tortured to agony." [29]

Natacha was cast firmly into the role of divorce perpetrator and Rudy's adoring public heaved all blame for the failed marriage on her. She did not bear the onslaught well. As she sought a path into her future, one leading far away from all things Hollywood and a disassociation from her life as Mrs. Rudolph Valentino, she grew morose over her wide-spreading negative reputation. George Wehner, as remedy, happened along at an opportune moment.

But was he a gifted psychic, an authentic medium as he claimed to be? Or was he an actor and opportunist who wielded his charm to exploit and engage the vulnerable? Was he a Rasputin, a Svengali who hypnotized and seduced the distraught Natacha Rambova into believing she needed his constant presence? How much of an influence did he have over her during that time of her life? Perhaps most intriguingly, did he predict the death of Natacha's beloved Rudolph Valentino?

Conversely, was it Natacha who beguiled George? Was he so impressed by her beauty, her cultured demeanor and social status that he abandoned his role as professional medium to become her companion and someone she relied on unequivocally? Who beguiled who? Who was George Wehner?

Chapter Four

A Trance Meeting

Seven years earlier, January 1918, in a house in the rural outskirts of Detroit, Michigan. George Wehner recalls,

"From the outside, the house looked dark and vacant. One would never dream of what was going on inside. This was managed so that no trouble might arise from the prying curious, or the police. It is against the law to take money for such services and at this séance a small fee was charged.

At last, after wary knocks at the door, we were let in. The séance was being held in a room upstairs kept specially for the purpose. The meeting had already begun, for we were late. I had not let my family know that I was coming here, for in spite of their interest they objected strenuously to my 'running about with spiritualists and fortune-tellers'. So in entering this forbidden house in this stealthy manner, I felt as the oppressed early Christians must have felt when they crept into their meeting places in the catacombs.

I shall never forget the moment when I entered that séance-room, nor the strange impression it made on me at the time. A faint reddish-glow spread dimly through a good-sized room, allowing me to see the vague outlines of people seated in two large semi-circles, one circle within the other. A droning murmur filled the room and swept out into the hall. With bended heads they were saying the Lord's Prayer.

Into this roseate twilight I stole and found a seat on a bench against the wall. After my eyes adapted themselves to the light, I saw before me against the opposite wall, a cabinet or sort of closet hung with purple curtains. Someone appeared to be sitting within this recess, for two knees and two shoes protruded from the curtains and from time to time a deep sigh issued from the spot. This, I later discovered, was a man who was developing materialization. In front of the cabinet and facing the semi-circles sat Mrs. Tixier, the medium who conducted the development.

When the prayer was finished, the séance sitters broke into singing a spiritualist hymn. All through this singing I had the most beautiful but fleeting glimpse of snow-white wisps of mist-like substance that went floating swiftly through the room. Misty, half-formed figures emerged from the cabinet and appeared suddenly in the midst of the sitters and some came gliding uncannily through the walls.

A few of these wraiths showed remarkably clear features but most of them were indistinct and full of ghastly holes caused by a lack of power to draw to themselves a sufficient quantity of atoms from the medium and the sitters. None of them appeared to linger but passed rapidly through the walls, ceiling and floor and many seemed to disintegrate in the air before our eyes.

Everyone in the room did not see these manifestations with the same degree of plainness. The inner eye was unopened in some. Now and then there were exclamations of wonder as several saw the same thing simultaneously. Some no doubt will think these people were hypnotized by Mrs. Tixier, or by themselves under repeated and strong suggestions. But I know that neither conclusion in this instance would be correct. I, myself, plainly saw the spirits standing behind or beside their mediums, concentrating upon them with the purpose to control." [30]

George Benjamin Wehner and Natacha Rambova, neé Winifred Shaughnessy and nicknamed "Wink", did not come from similar backgrounds. She was born in 1897 in Salt Lake City, Utah to a Mormon mother and her second husband, the Irish Catholic Colonel, Michael Shaughnessy. At the time of Natacha's birth, George Wehner was seven years old and living in Detroit, Michigan as the son of sculptor Carl Herman Wehner and painterly artist

Annie Haslett. According to his family, George demonstrated signs of psychic ability and fascination even as a child .

When he was an infant, his nanny performed a ritual on him she called her "Extraordinary Test". She held a crucifix before baby George and when he reached out to take hold of it, he reportedly gave it a "clear and knowing" look. This convinced the nanny he passed the "Extraordinary Test" thereby guaranteeing he would use his gift for good as a "knowing spirit".[31] The nanny assured the child's family this test proved his abilities were not spawned from any demonic forces.

George's one sibling, his sister Friedrieke, his mother, grandmother and aunts recalled his relating detailed accounts of sprites, fairies and elves he witnessed frolicking in the family pond. He regaled his wide-eyed family with tales of woodland creatures the size of his tiny thumb sailing the pond's waters on the back of turtles.

When George related such things to the women in his family, he received understanding and appreciation. His father, however, was horrified to hear such fantastical stories being acknowledged as truth and took his son to a doctor to see if he had a condition which could be cured.

George's grandmother would be the most influential in the development of his psychic abilities. She was a mystical woman who believed his visions and often encouraged him to tell her of his ethereal sightings. His other aunts did not discourage, with his Aunt Clara, a church organist, rewarding him with piano lessons.

To George and his sister Friede's dismay, their idyllic childhood in Detroit was interrupted when their mother and father moved the family to Newburgh-on-Hudson just north of New York City. There, George and Friede continued in their pastoral scamperings between their father's cavernous studio in the woods and the great home's green acres of lawn sprawling down the banks of the Hudson River.

When George was sixteen his beloved mother died and her grief-stricken husband Herman moved back to Detroit so his children could be raised by their grandmother and doting aunts. Herman Wehner encouraged George's musical talents to offset his unsettling obsession with spirits, fairies and the increasing presence of someone he referred to as White Cloud.

George would later claim that as a teenager he channeled an operetta aided entirely by White Cloud, as he was then unable to transcribe music. His father submitted this four-act psychic operetta

26

titled, "The Delight of Life" to the Michigan Conservatory of Music in 1908. "White Cloud's" score earned George a full scholarship and his relieved father believed this would provide a rational career direction for his son and deter him from pursuing any further interest in the occult.

While George attended the Michigan Conservatory of Music, Natacha's mother divorced Michael Shaughnessy and moved to San Francisco with her little daughter, Wink. The child passed her infancy and early childhood in the city by the bay; lonely with no siblings. By eight years of age, her mother married her third husband, Edgar DeWolfe. At a family gathering, DeWolfe was rough-housing with his new step-daughter and she reportedly fought back too furiously. The incident prompted her immediate enrollment in Leatherhead Court, a private girl's school outside of London. Wink would live in exile at Leatherhead Court for the remainder of her childhood.

There she spent her youthful years cloistered, living out her childhood fantasies through books primarily on mythology and ancient history. She left Leatherhead Court only to attend an occasional performance of the London Ballet or to travel to Paris for her summer vacations. In Paris she resided with her Aunt Elsie DeWolfe in her palatial residence in Versailles, the Villa Trianon. Just as George Wehner's artistic aesthetic was forged by doting aunts, the same could be said of Natacha.

However, George's aunts resided in suburban Detroit as working class women living within modest means. Natacha's Aunt Elsie lived in a palace of historical note where she ensured her niece's summers were rich in cultural inspiration; even studying ballet at the Paris Opera Ballet School with prima donna Roseta Mauri y Segura.[32]

When Natacha reached the age of seventeen, she left Leatherhead Court to return to America and pursue studying ballet with Russian emigré Theodore Kosloff by joining his Imperial Russian Ballet in New York City. She would live with her Aunt Teresa Werner who acted for a while as chaperone.

While George studied composition, theory and taught harmony at the Michigan Conservatory of Music, Natacha began touring the country with Kosloff's Russian ballet troupe. It was Kosloff who bestowed the Russian name "Natacha Rambova" on his student

Winifred and despite her being then underage at seventeen, she and Kosloff became romantically involved.

When Muzzie learned Kosloff had bedded her teen-age daughter, she threatened to have him deported back to Russia. Kosloff responded by sending Natacha into hiding. She traveled through Canada to England where she would live with Kosloff's estranged wife until her eighteenth birthday. It was then Muzzie, Kosloff and Natacha negotiated a resolution. Kosloff and his young lover Natacha would move to Los Angeles where he would open a school of ballet, pursue a career in the movies and collaborate with director Cecil B. Demille.

As a result of Kosloff's many infidelities with other members of his dance troupe, Natacha eventually decided to leave him. This proved to be a mission impossible as Kosloff was possessive to a violent degree. Upon hearing of her departure, he shot her in the leg with a hunting rifle as she climbed through a kitchen window to make her escape. The wound was not life-threatening but the injury effectively ended her dancing career.

While Natacha recovered from the buckshot wound to her thigh, in Detroit, the Michigan Conservatory of Music was declaring bankruptcy. This misfortune initiated George's turn to the military. He was rejected active service in the first World War and instead found employment as a piano player with Jessie Bonstelle's vaudeville stock company at the Garrick Theater.

During the First World War, he was also employed in the Dodge Ordinance War Plant, hired to write copy for promotional literature dispersed to boost morale and entice enlistment in the war effort. The monotony of a desk job shattered George's sensitive soul and he decided to leave Michigan for New York City to explore more open-minded territory where he would be free to pursue deep-trance mediumship as his life's work.

While a hungry George Wehner roamed the streets of Manhattan in search of any employment, Natacha lived in Hollywood, promoting her career as an art, set and costume designer with actress and producer Alla Nazimova. Rebounding from her ill-fated love affair with Theodore Kosloff she would meet, fall in love with and marry the man who would soon be known as "The Sheik" and "The Great Lover", Rudolph Valentino.

While Rudolph Valentino and his wife Natacha Rambova achieved their pinnacle of fame and fortune as husband and wife, George lived as a starving artist barely able to afford his weekly boarding house room rent. He often ate only through the generosity of his landlady and found sporadic work in a few vaudeville shows as a piano player and actor playing bit parts in skits.

His dream of earning a living as a medium did not, at that time, put a morsel of food on his plate. In search of the almighty dollar, he frequented the offices of sheet music publishers and the back stages of New York's prominent theaters; composing songs, music and lyrics in the hope of scoring just one hit. All the while he spoke openly about his mediumistic abilities and this did earn him a budding reputation as someone adept at giving a psychic reading.

George survived those thin times primarily because he was a prolific musical genius and consequently it was not long before one of his many ditties afforded him welcome reward. His hit song would spark his steady social climb and launch his career as a medium.

In 1921, George collaborated with fellow songwriter Louis Breau to write the lyrics for, "I Want my Mammy". The song touched the sentimental with its pining for a lost or distant mother and the lilting, catchy melody was soon being hummed from sea to shining sea.

Just as Rudolph Valentino's signature film, *The Sheik* was playing in theaters across the country in the fall of 1921, George's "I Want My Mammy" was being listened to on radios and recorded by performers eager to capitalize on the song's popularity. The song was most famously recorded by Eddie Cantor but there were various versions of the song including interpretations by Irving Kaufman, the Peerless Quartet and the Green Brothers Novelty Band. The song was also a popular selling roll for player pianos.[33] All of the renditions sold well and at last some coin jingled in George's thread-bare pockets. The successful "I Want My Mammy" brought him not only fortune but fame.

As George rode this wave of success by ingratiating himself into the New York theater and music scene, Rudolph Valentino became more idolized than any other star in the brief history of Hollywood. His wife Natacha achieved eminence at his side as a fashion icon known for her signature turbans and braids and the gorgeous couple's photographs appeared on the cover of every fan magazine with tabloid and gossip columnists trolling their every move.

It is certain George passed many a New York news stand broadcasting the latest about Rudolph Valentino and his wife Natacha Rambova and it is reasonable to assume he heard their mention. But he was then preoccupied with launching his own career in New York as a medium for the rich and famous.

By cleverly marketing his psychic wares, his calendar filled with requests for séances and with each booking, he made it known he was anxious for the next introduction. "I Want My Mammy" was his introduction into the public's acknowledgment and approval but his vision of success was not then musical.

He dined with Dorothy Benjamin Caruso, Enrico Caruso's widow, conducted séances for movie star Doris Kenyon, Broadway actress Amelia Bingham, actresses Minnie Maddern Fiske, Janet Beecher, Mrs. Harry Bamberger and many members of the American Society for Psychical Research. Besieged by calls for psychic readings and séances, George's dreamed-of career took off.

The timing of his successful self-promotion was flawless. Séances were then considered entertaining after-dinner activity and this soon translated into his comfortable Manhattan lifestyle. Perhaps his success was in great measure due to a shrewd inclusion in his séance process. He knew most of his clientele were also involved in the increasingly popular theosophical movement. What better way to gain their attention than to expound upon the one subject of which they were already avid devotees.

In his role as medium, George would not only be conducting séances, but acting as point man for the founder of theosophy, Helena Petrovna Blavatsky. He soon claimed she was one of his spirit guides and White Cloud would be sharing the duties from the astral plane. George's professional affiliation with theosophy and this deceased Russian woman provided him with a winning combination, a fait accompli and earned him the unwavering devotion of a faithful following, most notably Natacha Rambova.

Chapter Five

The Dead Russian Woman

When Helena Petrovna Blavatsky died in 1891, she was world-renown as the founder of the Theosophical Society and traveling with an entourage of scribes and scholars; one of them being her secretary Claude Falls Wright. Blavatsky spent her life psychically channeling lengthy arcane doctrines she alleged were revealed to her from etheric master guides or mahatmas. This is the method she used to write her life's manifesto, *The Secret Doctrine,* which became the bible of theosophists championing her work.

The tenets of her theosophical thought were far from dogmatic and never constituted a religious practice. She based her teachings and writings on a broad analysis of religions and spiritualism while searching for commonality in all aspects of the religious experience and cosmic order.

Blavatsky's cosmically expanded history of humankind was unique in that it provided an intriguing new aspect to religion; the occult. This appealed to the religiously disenfranchised as well as to spiritualists. Blavatsky left a flourishing world organization of theosophical societies whose focus at that time included occult practices.

Her original design was to found theosophy as a synthesis of all religions, occult beliefs, philosophies and mystical practices throughout the world. However lofty her aspirations, her philosophies became the subject of controversy and some were

31

eventually rejected when it was alleged her discussions of the hierarchy of race contributed to Nazi ideology.

The emphasis on the occult in Blavatsky's doctrines would wane over the years and eventually be eliminated from theosophic doctrine. However, in 1925, Blavatsky's word on such subjects as the astral plane, communication with the dead and the construct of the after-life were still integrated within her theosophic tradition. This became the focus of George Wehner's séances.

He alleged he was born on Blavatsky's birthday and claimed his father experienced a vision of her importance in his son's life. It seemed predestined George would adopt Blavatsky as an influential spirit guide.

George's process as a medium allowed for the presence of several spirit guides to speak through him. Every member of his cast of the discarnate, including White Cloud and Helena Blavatsky held their unique role, such as Frank, who before his death was George's friend in Detroit. Frank was a musician in his earth-life and it was his spirit who whistled before George went into a trance. There were also lesser guides; gypsies, deceased relatives and even historical figures.

Yet, throughout most of George's life it was White Cloud who dominated his séance process and acted as host by summoning and introducing spirits during a séance. This was the case when White Cloud introduced Helena Blavatsky, or H.P.B., as he referred to her.

From her first introduction, H.P.B. became George's preeminent spirit guide. By the time he began conducting séances for Natacha Rambova, Muzzie and the Bamberger Circle of Saturday Nighters, White Cloud's role seemed primarily to summon H. P. Blavatsky.

For this reason George encouraged his clientele to study theosophy and pursue this as a meaningful adjunct to his séances. He befriended and cultivated relationships with prestigious members of the New York Theosophical Society and utilized his séances to advance the study of Blavatsky's doctrines. Many of his messages from the other side were lectures on theosophy delivered in the voice of its founder.

In this way, George convinced those studying Blavatsky's *Secret Doctrine* they were communicating with "H.P.B." and she was speaking directly to them via his body which he vacated for her use by means of a deep trance. With White Cloud making the introduction, H.P.B. did not disappoint and left her audiences of sitters in George's séances sated not only with mystical messages from the astral plane but with esoteric wisdom.

By early 1926, George was conducting several séances a week for Natacha in which he imparted no small amount of theosophical doctrine directly from the movement's founder. From the understanding of Zen and Buddhist practices to levitation and telepathic communication, no subject seemed out of his Blavatsky-inspired boundaries.

శ్రీ

The parlor of theosophist Leslie Grant Scott's Manhattan penthouse resembled a Louis Quartorze ballroom; polished, cavernous and appointed with European and American Victorian furniture.[34] Leslie's husband, Reginald Thomas Maitland Scott, known by his pen name, R.T.M. Scott, was a best-selling author of popular pulp crime and action novels which were rich in theosophical and paranormal plot lines.

R.T.M. Scott was born in Malaysia and as he spent his childhood in exotic locales, he drew upon his own experiences in writing his books. Some of his more successful novels were his Aurelius Smit series; Smit being a sleuth similar to Sir Arthur Conan Doyle's detective Sherlock Holmes. It was while R.T.M. was working in India that he met and fell in love with Leslie Grant. They married and had one child, a son, R.T.M. Junior.

The commercial popularity of R.T.M.'s novels permitted them to live in splendor in Manhattan and furnish their home as an unparalleled showcase replete with a baby grand piano, velvet draperies and baroque art in heavy gold-leafed frames. Installed as the famous couple's most impressive artifact; a reproduction oil painting of Rafael's Madonna; *La Madonna della Seggiola*, "The Madonna of the Chair".[35]

R.T.M. and Leslie Grant Scott were influential members of the New York Theosophical Society and Leslie revered as a high-ranking scholar. The focus of her expertise was Blavatsky's *Secret Doctrine* and for this she was known as a prestigious instructor. It was logical Natacha would seek out Leslie Scott to further her theosophical education. When Leslie began mentoring Natacha, she and her husband R.T.M. were hosting regular séances conducted by George Wehner.

It was during one séance in the Scott's parlor, attended by Natacha and other Saturday Nighters, when George stunned the sitters with a prophecy. As the last refrains of the Lord's Prayer were said, George sat mouth gaped, tongue thrust forward, eyes closed, his head rolling left to right.

Leslie, R.T.M. and their guests sat in silence waiting for George's whistling to begin and then that moment of silence before White Cloud would begin his introductions. In this séance, White Cloud made no introductions but instead began recounting a scene he seemed to be witnessing by saying,

"The great man on boat falls in water."

George sways in his chair as the sitters lean forward wondering what he could be talking about. White Cloud speaks louder.

"Mr. Wright is in black water. They turn boat away." White Cloud gasps in the darkened room calling out, "Crocodiles!"

Leslie Grant was seated a few feet away from George when she heard the name "Mr. Wright" and knew to whom White Cloud was referring. The moment George came out of his trance she rushed to telephone Eleanor Broenniman. She asked if she had spoken to George about Claude Wright's disappearance in Nicaragua. Eleanor assured Leslie, not a word.

Eleanor Broenniman booked a immediate séance with George. White Cloud relayed much the same account to Eleanor and it was then she booked the trip to Nicaragua with her son Edgar. She impressed on George how it would be of great value to her, to the family of Claude Wright and to the New York Theosophical Society if he would accompany her and Edgar on the sail to Nicaragua.

George accepted this invitation and informed Natacha of his imminent departure. Hearing the unwelcome news she lamented,

"I shall be sick with worry, George. You are not suited for such primitive adventure."

"Natacha," George reassured, "I am all the adventurer required for such a journey. You are not to worry as that might compromise the spiritual nature of my work for Eleanor."

"Then you will agree to accompany me to France with Aunt Teresa when you return?"

"Of course, Natacha. We shall sail for France."

The truth was, George would worry about Natacha because he knew she still grieved Rudy's absence. He witnessed her despair upon hearing her mother's account of how Rudy paid a visit to the chateau over the Christmas holiday. Muzzie spared her daughter no detail as she relayed how Rudy spent time alone in the bedroom he shared with Natacha at the chateau and how he laid his head on her lap and sobbed.[36]

Throughout, Natacha remained outwardly resolute. When her divorce from Rudy became law on her birthday, January 19th, she gave every public indication she was thrilled to be done being Rudolph Valentino's wife. She granted a testy interview with the headline, "Miss Rambova Desires That The World Forget She Was Valentino's Wife,"

"Interrupted while taking voice lessons at her home, the former Mrs. Valentino was reluctant to talk about her marriage to Rudy or her divorce from him,
'I have no desire to say mean things about Mr. Valentino. If he wants to talk, that is his privilege. I want the world to forget that I ever was his wife. My whole life will be devoted to my career'..."

When the reporter asked if she would discuss her marriage, she answered,

"Why no. What a foolish question. I told you I was not interested in Mr. Valentino didn't I? I think the country is pretty well fed up with stories about us anyway.' "[37]

During that winter of her discontent, Natacha promoted her stage ambitions by appearing in a production of the play, *The Purple Vial* which opened in theaters in New England in January. On February 8, the short thriller opened at the Palace Theater in New York. The drama was referred to as a "playlet" and received reviews which more often than not were reports on the status of her marriage and divorce. In nearly every theater where *The Purple Vial* opened, management arranged to show one of Rudy's movies. This infuriated Natacha and she refused to appear on stage unless another movie was shown. In Hartford, Connecticut, the theater billed a showing of *Cobra* until Natacha intervened with her ultimatum.

"I'll not appear in this theater on the same program with one of my husband's pictures. You either change the picture or get another vaudeville act." [38]

Despite her full schedule and promising stage career, it was with trepidation Natacha said good-bye to George when he left for

Central America with Edgar and Eleanor Broenniman. She knew the voyage could benefit a prestigious member of the theosophic society and she was as eager as anyone else who attended the prophetic séance to see what George could discover about the mysterious disappearance of Claude Falls Wright.

She resigned to counting the days and weeks until the end of March when George would return. With her fondest wishes of farewell bestowed, George boarded the train for New Orleans.

Natacha was left behind in Manhattan to cope in the absence of the astral advice of Helena Blavatsky or George's etheric counsel and feeling captive on her earth-bound plane.

Chapter Six

Its Elemental

Pearl Lagoon, Nicaragua, March 1926.

The windows of the Monrovian Mission rattle as the beams of the old building creak from the straining. George clutches a bed post and struggles to maintain footing. This is his first earthquake! He lurches towards the window to see small houses crumbling, people screaming through the streets, livestock running amok and flocks of birds screeching skyward. The chaos induces trance and clairvoyance in George; as if he is part of an ancient dance.

"Suddenly the mission began to rock and shake back and forth violently and there was the sound of smashing china and falling objects. I heard Mrs. Broenniman scream in some other part of the building...

After my first shock of surprise passed I saw many spirits of ancient Indians dancing in circles exultantly as though delighted with the shaking of the ground. I knew they were ancient because of their scanty clothing and headdresses. And malignant-looking elementals appeared among them waving their arms and legs and rolling about on the ground as if in malicious glee..."[39]

George wonders if these elementals caused the earthquake in retaliation to the appearance of white people. Had the Broennimans and his presence in Pearl Lagoon instigated this catastrophe?

That very afternoon, Eleanor, Edgar and George embark on their return to New York; departing amidst the earthquake's devastation. They board a small banana freighter headed back to New Orleans with George calming a frightened spider monkey perched on his shoulder.

The seas to New Orleans were rough and George would attribute his surviving the awful ordeal to the grateful monkey who recovered quickly to entertain him throughout.

In New York City, Natacha did not fare well in George's absence. She was still besieged by prying press and still close in thought to Rudy with time not healing the wound. Snide columnists filled their column inches with insinuation and snarky comments about her while sharing the latest scoop on Rudy's nightlife and his dates with some of Hollywood's most beautiful movie stars; most notably Pola Negri.

Natacha grew anxious with the news and her bitterness in coping was apparent to those around her. Rudy's popularity was raging, women clambering for his arm and his blockbuster film, *The Eagle* opening to stellar reviews. Natacha tried and failed to keep her mind off the sore subject.

By March, Rudy had returned triumphant to Los Angeles to prepare for filming *The Son of the Sheik* and it was obvious to Muzzie, Aunt Teresa and George Wehner that Natacha was still very much in love with her ex-Sheik. They also believed he was still in love with her.

To them, their divorce appeared to be more of a destructive force in both Rudy and Natacha's lives than their rocky marriage had ever been. He was reportedly drinking heavily and spending his nights in speakeasies to then sleep all day and repeat. It was rumored he looked exhausted and appeared bloated, even overweight. Heartache had the opposite effect on Natacha. She lost weight, became high-strung and over-active. This pained her loved ones and consequently her reliance on her erstwhile psychic George was not discouraged.

In his devotion to the woebegone Natacha, he shielded her from all negativity; especially news of Rudy's love life. This was hardly an unpleasant task for George as Natacha was after all a gorgeous, twenty-nine year old woman immersed in a world of New York's wealthiest theosophical notables.

By day, Natacha vanquished her sorrowful internal monologue by hurrying about Manhattan while acting, writing, sketching and designing. By night, she covered the parlor lamps with scarves to create an amber light to prowl about in the after-life seeking solace from the dead.

By May, divorce had brought Natacha no peace of mind and her bouts of melancholy concerned her loved ones. In a fight or flight quandary, she felt the French Riviera might resolve her quest to establish distance from her ex-husband's latest success and his budding romance with Pola Negri.

George's evening séances provided her escape by blurring the line between a painful present and the dreamy ectoplasm of the here-after. The astral plane seduced Natacha's fragile psyche and as the date of the sail for Europe approached, George seldom left her side. In less emotionally perilous times her loved ones might have encouraged less of a dependency on a medium and direct her towards a more earth-bound recovery. As Natacha walked her razor's edge that spring, no one in her world made a move to intervene.

At last the day of departure arrived. Natacha, Aunt Teresa, George, a squadron of little dogs, including a recently-welcomed King Charles pup [40] and the excitable monkey boarded the *Homeric* for LaHavre, France. George felt whatever they lacked in dignity as a result of their pets' chaos, they compensated for in fun. Although every puppy passed the Atlantic crossing sick as dogs, the monkey thrived at sea and regaled them all by leaping in and out of the portholes.

This was George's first trip to Europe and he was euphoric with anticipation. It was on the first day of the crossing he resolved to remedy Natacha's heavy heart. For George it was exhilarating to head into open sea as he watched the New York City skyline fade over the horizon. The Atlantic swept him into a state of psychic illumination as the sea air and the sensation of the *Homeric* churning through the deep conspired to imbue George with unusual exuberance.

He wished Natacha shared the same buoyant energy he enjoyed and this desire inspired his initiative; his opening gesture being fragrant flowers delivered to Natacha's stateroom each morning.

With every nod of understanding he bestowed cosmic comfort on the emotionally frail Natacha. Evening séances were held in her stateroom and as the great ship rolled into the waves, George summoned H.P.B. and the reassuring voice of White Cloud. With the fragrance of his days' blooms as incense, George held forth.

His promenades on deck provided him with more psychic inspiration and there he alleged he witnessed oracles and omens. He would relate news of these spectacles to a rapt Natacha while she took copious notes, illustrating them with sketches.

George envisioned air and sea elementals churning as cloud formations or waves and manifesting in fantastical forms both benign and menacing. A vision of the head of a great lion roared from the vapors over the ship and a winged dragon hovered over him, hissed and disappeared in an instant. Natacha recorded George's sightings, including his discovery of one elemental in the form of a writhing octopus which washed up on deck. For George, these were all omens to be interpreted.

Natacha did not question. Although she was a believer and his scribe, she was not unaware George might be altering his reports depending on her mood. If she was in an optimistic mood, his accounts were light, even humorous. If she was gloomy, he delivered sermons of sympathy and empowerment, assuring her these sea elementals were a positive portend of a new phase of her life. All happiness awaited.

Throughout George's trans-Atlantic mediumship, the voice of Helena Blavatsky continued speaking with Natacha. H.P.B. advised her to rise into the realms of higher vibrational thought patterns and focus on her lessons in Buddhism, Taoism and the theosophic synthesis of all.

By the time George debarked to set first foot in France with Natacha, Aunt Teresa and the menagerie, he felt secure in his summer residency on the Côte D'Azur. Natacha would not be far away from him, morning, noon and moonlit Mediterranean night. He had handily won over the matriarch Muzzie and her sister Teresa but he had yet to meet Richard Hudnut. Convincing the Hudnut patriarch of his other-worldy powers might prove more challenging.

Muzzie welcomed George to Paris as if he were visiting royalty and by the time they settled into their rooms at the Hotel Majestic on the Avenue Kleber, she was already informing her friends in Paris and on the Riviera all about the young American medium's arrival.

"...Now began a period rich in psychic experiences with earth-bound souls and with memory-pictures glimpsed in the astral light of old palaces and chateaux at Versailles, Fontainbleau, the lovely district of the Loire..." [41]

George's first European experience was all the more pleasurable as Natacha at last seemed content. This was most apparent when visiting her Aunt Elsie DeWolfe. Natacha walked the familiar, echoing halls and aromatic gardens of her Aunt Elsie's, Villa Trianon and appeared to join the living. The Villa Trianon had been her summer home throughout her lonely childhood at Leatherhead Court and those childhood memories revived her in joyful reception.

Aunt Elsie DeWolfe hosted a grand soireé for her visitors from America where they dined on pheasant while chatting with French cultural elite under the chic striped canvas awnings of the Villa Trianon's terraces. George was wined on the finest wines and dined on epicurean delicacies and any memory of his hungry days on the streets of Manhattan faded and forever.

While in Paris, he continued to keep any news about Rudolph Valentino from Natacha and often diverted her from passing newspaper stands in the street. Still, he read the headlines and knew Rudy had completed filming *The Son of the Sheik* and that he and manager Ullman planned to train east from Los Angeles to New York to promote the film. George would always seize his moments to share Rudy's news with Natacha with caution in order to keep her apprised with minimal distress.

The stay in Paris was brief as Natacha was eager to head south to Juan les Pins. She'd enjoyed so many happy times there with Rudy, her loved ones wondered whether this visit for her was a good or a very bad idea. She still worried openly to them about her ex-husband; was he smoking too much or drinking bad whiskey? She had, on a few occasions, even composed love letters which were crumpled and thrown away.

With the summer of 1926 about to bear down with its heat and humidity on both continents, Rudy would swelter on a train heading for New York City and Natacha would board a train south from a steamy Paris with her small zoo and entourage, headed towards those cool Mediterranean breezes.

Chapter Seven

Destination Mystère en Côte D'Azur

The train station in Juan les Pins, France, summer 1926.

Richard Hudnut's chauffeur is dozing when he hears the whistle of the "Train Bleu" arriving from the Gare de Lyon in Paris. He reaches for his cap on the dashboard, exits the great vehicle and strides along the concrete walkway along side the railroad tracks. The train screeches to its halt, steam billowing. As the passengers begin to disembark, he cranes his neck to see Natacha.

With limited room in the limousine, he anticipates driving the five minutes from the station up to the chateau several times. When the chauffeur sees Natacha, Muzzie, Aunt Teresa and George appear with five puppies straining on the end of their leashes and a squealing monkey, he can only grumble through his formal nods while situating his passengers.

The limousine lumbers on its way and heads into a turn up the hill onto the Rue Chemin du Crouton, a street lined with towering palms. George sits silently in the back seat, absorbing the vibrational energy of the new terrain. He senses a calm enhanced by the sea air and even his monkey seems unusually tranquilized. The rarefied locale with its pink and white stuccoed homes is nestled in shrubbery and blooming bougainvillea providing a privacy only the greatest wealth can afford. Within a few minutes the chateau's iron gate swings into its slow open.

The limousine's approach provides the drama for George as this is his first view of the chateau; the twenty-four room manse and unarguably the most impressive residence in Juan les Pins.

The pups make the first and fast entrance, skittering across the polished marble floor of the chateau's foyer. Richard Hudnut steps forward to shake George's hand giving a laugh at the monkey perched on his shoulder. George's first impression of Richard Hudnut, or "Uncle Dickie", is that of reserved gentleman yet psychically skeptical.

George absorbs his initial impressions and the spiritual emanations from the auspicious home; the baroque antiques, tapestries with long histories from the early Seventeenth Century and gilded Louis XV and XVI furniture. These treasures, for him, are still alive with memories of decades gone by. He senses a satisfying affinity with the Riviera, the chateau and its summer inhabitants.

"The Hudnut chateau is filled with treasures; old Gobelin tapestries, collections of jade and ambers and lovely old furniture upholstered in Saint Cyr needlepoint in mellowed colors. There are enormous Savonnerie rugs of great beauty of color and design. All of these things hallowed by the breath of time give forth a vibrational quality that makes for an unusually psychic atmosphere." [42]

Muzzie whisks George into a tour of the chateau interiors, swanning though the library with its Louis XV armchairs upholstered in pale blue damask.[43] Then it is on to a sitting room with a marble fire-place; in each room the walls are appointed with art ranging in period and style from modern portraiture to ancient artifact including works by Rousseau, Filippo Lippi and Peter Paul Rubens. [44]

Muzzie's tour culminates in an exit through the rear of the chateau and the revelation of the Court of Palms. There a fountain gushes a sparkling waterfall which takes George's breath away. He stands by the cascade to solemnify the moment, facing the panorama of the Mediterranean below.

It was with a sense of great purpose he unpacked that evening to settle into his summer residency. As a crimson sun set over the distant haze of the mountains of Estérel, the sitting parlor with adjoining terrace was prepared for his first séance at the chateau. Most of the room's furniture had been removed, all but a round table and positioned chairs. The lights were dimmed and the heavy draperies drawn and high on the wall loomed the imposing portrait of Helena Petrovna Blavatsky as executed by the renown Yugoslavian court painter and Hudnut friend, Paul Ivanovitch.

George took his seat before the sitters, Uncle Dickie, Muzzie, Aunt Teresa and Natacha; the only sound being a single nightingale warbling its evening song on the terrace.

As George began delivering his evening messages from the astral plane, he was already breaking news among the French Riviera's elite.

During the summer of 1926, a colony of wealthy Americans populated the prestigious residences along the French Riviera known as the Côte d'Azur. The Mediterranean Sea was not the only force inspiring American royalty to call those hillside estates their homes. The casinos in Monte Carlo, Nice and Marseilles provided an opportunity to parade as high society in their glittering gowns and jewelry. The summer crowd reveled in the aroma of rosemary, lavender and pine as well as the balm of their own wealth. This was their ultimate destination.

The French Riviera status conscious were intrigued to hear news of the handsome, eccentric psychic from New York and of course those séances being held at the Hudnut chateau. They did not comprise a large community of Americans but their comings and goings were the topics of daily chats in the morning cafés and during their evening promenades. George Wehner was a new bauble to be fawned over and his etheric connections on the astral plane rendered him irresistible.

When Natacha and Muzzie introduced him to their gold-plated friends, séances were scheduled in villas, castles and chateaux from Monaco to Antibes. George became a regular guest at the Villa Margueritas in Monaco, the home of Cora Brown Potter of Chicago. Known by her stage name, Mrs. Brown Potter, she was an American who made her name in British theater after separating from her coffee broker tycoon husband. Mrs. Cora Brown mingled with British royalty and any invitation to her villa was coveted by the Riviera's rich and famous. George charmed Mrs. Cora Brown and handily won the hearts of many of the American ladies of the Côte d'Azur. He would even convince the modern dancer Loie Fuller of his powers by foretelling a strong-arm robbery on her Paris estate.

He dabbled in watercolors and entertained by psychically locating antiques; envisioning the objects d'art and conveniently including the address of the dealer holding the prize. He also developed a close friendship with Paul Ivanovitch. The sixty-seven year old painter was also engaged at the chateau during the summer of 1926; having been commissioned to paint portraits of Uncle Dickie, Muzzie, Natacha and George.

Throughout June and July, George remained focused on Natacha and took his cues from whatever she seemed preoccupied with each day. His diligence in protecting her from news about Rudy was sincere but she nevertheless found copies of *Le Figaro* left about the chateau by her step-father. She knew Rudy was in New York and her attentiveness to this fact made it obvious there could not be enough distance between them for Natacha not to care.

Her loved ones at the chateau did their best to prevent Natacha from finding those news items and maids swept up Uncle Dickie's morning paper if they heard her coming their way. Despite, Natacha felt compelled to know and if she found a newspaper she scoured the pages in a search of any tidbit.

She stayed abreast of Rudy's news as he and Ullman promoted *The Son of the Sheik* and as he became the victim of the libelous Pink Powder Puff editorial attributing effeminacy in American men to his influence. She followed the drama of Rudy's response to the anonymously written editorial and again and again she expressed worry to her loved ones saying perhaps Rudy was smoking too much and drinking questionable whiskey.

On Monday, August 16th, her fears realized when a cablegram arrived at the chateau from George Ullman. Muzzie read the cablegram aloud to a wide-eyed Natacha. Rudy was in the Polyclinic Hospital in Manhattan, having fallen ill from complications from a perforated ulcer and was about to have surgery. Ullman added that Rudy requested the cable be sent to Natacha to express his love and assurances all would be well. She was not to worry.

Natacha's immediate response was to cable her love to Rudy sharing all best wishes from his loved ones at the chateau. She then retreated with George to seek answers via séance. She placed Rudy's cablegram on the round table in the H.P.B. room and stared at the message from New York as if in doing so she kept her line to Rudy open and direct. Despite everyone's reassurances of Rudy's robust health and his sure and prompt recovery, Natacha panicked. The

45

cablegram left no doubt about her course of action and she told George they would return to New York immediately.

The arrival of Rudy's next cablegram was anxiously awaited and Natacha cabled him a second time sending more love. For a brief while, a glimmer of hope was evident for that overly-pondered reunion between Rudy and Natacha. With the cablegram in hand expressing Rudy's love, Natacha was no longer ambivalent and openly discussed the reconciliation with Rudy. Their divorce, she admitted, had been a mistake.

By Wednesday evening the mood at the chateau was optimistic with the consensus being that Rudy was healing and his crisis had passed. Surely there would be more encouraging news from Ullman in New York in the morning. After dinner and the adjournment to the terrace, Uncle Dickie, Muzzie, Aunt Teresa, Natacha and George watch a champagne colored sunset, with Natacha's return to New York for Rudy's recovery lending a joyful tone to their conversation. As the H.P.B. room was being prepared, the medium recalled,

"... As usual before a séance, I began to grow extremely sensitive and to feel vibratory emanations from my surroundings. I felt the pressing nearness of another world and the penetrating intermingling of the auras of souls passed on. Then one came nearer who brushed repeatedly against the astral antenna of my nerves and prompted me with an almost overwhelming desire to express his eager messages..." [45]

The familiar nightingale warbles on the terrace as Muzzie drapes veils over the side lights and the séance sitters take their seats in their familiar circle. Natacha seems irritated,

"Never before have I heard a bird sing like that," she says, "I'm going to close the windows. I can't stand it. It makes me think of the Hollywood days with Rudy." [46]

With the windows latched shut, Natacha returns to her seat. As Muzzie begins to recite the Lord's Prayer, the Mistral winds gust, sending dried palm fronds scraping across the terrace. For George the atmosphere in the room that Wednesday evening is charged with astral currents and he witnesses dim, ghostly figures crowding into the room and moving through the ethers.

"As I looked about the circle I could not help comparing the two kinds of living personalities in the room, the living alive and the living dead! Richard Hudnut, at seventy, serenely charming and debonair, Mrs. Hudnut, Muzzie, with her red-gold hair and eyes of pale jade, Natacha, calm and stately in emerald and gold lame, her finely chiseled features and dark eyes set off by a turban of vermilion - and then, these astral visitors so dim to our perceptions, yet more real and tangibly enduring than any of us on earth." [47]

The nightingale on the terrace can still be heard over the wind and its persistence feels ominous to George. He sinks into his chair with eyes closed, his breathing growing shallow.

In a moment he begins his whistle but in a strange harmony with the bird's muffled song. His whistling stops and George sits silently surrendering his body to the spirits. For a few minutes he speaks rapidly in a garble of voices; children, men, some loud and some murmurs. [48]

Natacha defies the decorum and interrupts, "I felt an icy wind blow through the room. Did anyone else notice it?"

"I felt it just now, yes," says Muzzie.

Uncle Dickie adds, "The room *is* growing darker,"

George speaks directly to Natacha in a man's voice; a man with an Italian accent.

"Natacha, Natacha!' he calls out, "I knew you would come!" Natacha startles as the desperate voice sounds as if someone is trying to wake from a nightmare.

"What? You *knew* I would come?"

"I love you! I knew you would come back!" the voice speaks through George.

"But I don't understand," Natacha asks, "Come *where*?"

"New York."

"But, my dear friend," Muzzie interrupts, "Don't be foolish. This is not Manhattan. We are three thousand miles from there in the south of France."

George's head rolls from side to side as the voice seems to drift off repeating, "New York, New York, New York."

"I have never heard of such a thing," exclaims Muzzie sounding annoyed, "One would think..."

"Hush, Mother," says Natacha, "This is something unusual. Let him speak to me."

George intones, "Natacha, where are you? Where are you? Don't go away."

"Yes, I am Natacha and I won't go away. But, tell me please who you are."

"Rudy," the voice answers, "I knew you would come...I knew you would come."

Natacha's face grows visibly paler even in the darkened room.

Muzzie eyes her daughter's reaction. "Don't you think we should break the circle and bring the medium out of the trance?"

"No. Mother wait. There is something very strange going on here. That voice sounds almost exactly like Rudy's."

George's body begins to twitch. He brushes his hand against his face saying,

"Natacha, cara mia," the voice then speaks in Italian.

Natacha replies in Italian.

After a few minutes, Aunt Teresa asks, "What is he saying? What?"

Natacha answers, "He seems to think we are in New York and I have come back to him. I can't understand it. It sounds like Rudy as if he were talking in his sleep."

Then a cry from George startles the sitters, "Jenny!"

"What does he mean by Jenny?" Aunt Teresa asks.

Natacha explains, "Jenny was June Mathis' mother, Virginia, who helped Rudy when he first came to Hollywood."

George then speaks in the voice of a woman, an older woman's voice repeating the name, "Gabriella, Gabriella."

Natacha asks, "Are you Rudy's mother?"

The frail voice answers, "Si, Gabriella." Gabriella goes on to explain how her son Rudolfo is ill in New York. In her frail voice she says her son will not recover and will pass on to return to her within a few days. [49]

Hearing this, the circle is broken and George is brought out of his trance. As much as they all want to dismiss the message from Rudy's mother, they all know George capable of prescient knowledge. He is told about the visitations from Rudy and Rudy's mother, Gabriella with Natacha insisting none of this can possibly be true.

Natacha cabled Rudy again on Thursday and Friday morning and was heartened by another cablegram and this one from him. He expressed his love for her and wrote he was keeping her first cablegram under his pillow.

By Friday, a cablegram arrived from Ullman reporting Rudy much improved and relaying news he was expected to leave the hospital within a few days. The chateau was abuzz with the talk of the perfect setting for Rudy's recovery, Natacha's imminent return to New York and their reunion. Muzzie suggested they retreat to the Hudnut mountain home in upstate New York, "Foxlair" saying the fall foliage in the Catskills and fresh air would be exactly what Rudy needed. Natacha felt Paris or London might provide them with more privacy and Aunt Teresa suggested they spend the fall in Juan les Pins and bring Rudy directly to the chateau. On that Friday, Natacha's love for Rudy turned back time, erasing her past year of misery without him.

The mood in the chateau that evening was one of optimism and they talked of little else but Rudy's recovery and the magnificent reconciliation. The chateau residents gathered for another séance to channel more good news via their medium. Seated once again around the table, Uncle Dickie, Muzzie, Aunt Teresa and Natacha, quieted into the ritual they had come to know well that summer.

On that Friday night there was no bird singing and despite Natacha's irritation with its persistence, its absence seemed more disturbing. That annoying nightingale which reminded Natacha of her life in Hollywood with Rudy was silent. Her heart pounded as she whispered the Lord's Prayer and waited for George to speak.

Chapter Eight

The Extraordinary Test

The H.P.B. room, the Hudnut chateau, Juan les Pins, Friday evening, August 20, 1926.

"In the name of the Father, the Son and the Holy Ghost, Amen."

Silence settles over the H.P.B. room as George stops whistling. He begins to speak and in the measured voice of an elderly man who identifies himself as Rudy's spirit guide Mesolope, the ancient Egyptian. Natacha startles with the revelation.

Mesolope delivers a lengthy message, sharing insights into Rudy's psychic achievements on earth and his spiritual significance. He speaks of Rudy's automatic writing and his deep trance ability, assuring them Rudy was truly an adept master of a high vibrational pattern. Mesolope expounds on Rudy's astral importance and how his effect on the world was a gift of great cosmic value. He seems as if he is trying to convince the sitters Rudy was already serving some cause in the great beyond.

"Mesolope told the eager group, in as gentle manner as possible, that the time of Rudy's stay on earth was up; that in spite of the reassuring news...received from America, Rudy would soon pass from his body." [50]

Uncle Dickie issues a snort of disbelief and Aunt Teresa and Muzzie watch Natacha sitting with her eyes closed. George then speaks in the voice of a different entity; a louder, stronger voice. He announces he is Rudy's spirit guide, Black Feather. The American Indian delivers a briefer message explaining how Rudy's great appeal manifested as the world's recognition of his eternal spirit. Black Feather says he would soon escort Rudy through his crossing over. The voice fades, saying he could not speak any longer as it was time for him to return to Rudy's side in New York. Natacha opens her eyes to stare into her lap, stifling sobs as not to jar George from his trance. George recalled the moment,

"Then Jenny came through. 'I have been with Rudy since his illness,' she said, 'I will be with him when the earthly end comes-and how joyfully I will meet him when he begins his life anew! You remember in the previous séance that he called out my name, Jenny! Well, I want you to remember what I am saying. It was at the time they were taking him to the hospital in the ambulance. I was in the ambulance by his side. He opened his eyes and cried out my name. Yes, his time is up, his work is finished and he will be with us in spirit within the next few days.' " [51]

The séance ends abruptly with everyone in tears. Natacha stumbles sobbing from the room with Muzzie bustling along side. Uncle Dickie makes an effort to reassure Aunt Teresa saying surely Rudy was young and in good health. He glares at George.

"Richard," George replies, "perhaps this is all wrong. Perhaps the spirits are playing morbid tricks on us and we will soon hear that Rudy has passed any danger."

"I am not so sure, George," Uncle Dickie rises from his chair to walk towards the terrace, "Mesolope and Black Feather had a great deal to say. "

"Go to Natacha, George, go!" Uncle Dickie then turns to open the great doors and step out into the night. He gazes down at the lights in the harbor, twinkling in the water's reflection. The street lamps flicker and the promenade is busy with cars and those strolling in their after-dinner. Uncle Dickie Hudnut is overcome with regret. Why did he allow this séance master to say such things? Why had he not intervened to silence him?

The following morning Natacha stood in the foyer with two cablegrams ready to be dispatched; one to George Ullman asking for more updates on Rudy's condition and another to Rudy expressing her deepest love for him. This cablegram was composed as the reversal of her last letter mailed somewhere crossing the prairie a year earlier. She wrote this cablegram as a long message of loving remorse in which she regretted their divorce and begged Rudy's every forgiveness. She assured him she would see him in New York within the next few weeks and that she would care for him throughout his recovery. The agonizing wait for Rudy's reply then set in.

When no cablegrams were delivered to the chateau on Sunday or on Monday, Natacha chain-smoked and paced in her bedroom. George stayed close, attempting to distract her with tales of the dogs' and the monkey's antics.

Monday evening, George noticed Natacha seemed to be giving way to the long wait. She took to bed and called George to her room to ask him if the smell of tuberoses signified a death.

"Yes, Natacha, I think that is the case. But why do you ask?"

"While I was setting my room just now to go to bed, I smelled them, the tuberoses so strong here in the room. It seemed to overpower me and I felt dizzy."

George sat down on the edge of her bed and leaned over to hold her in his arms as she wept saying, "I'm so frightened." [52]

On Tuesday morning, the cablegram arrived from New York telling of Rudy's death the previous day. Uncle Dickie delivered the news. On hearing the crushing finality of that cablegram, Natacha rushed to collapse in her mother's arms screaming, "No! No! No!" Muzzie led her keening daughter to her bed knowing any consolation to be futile. Natacha curled into her bed covers and through sobs called out to Rudy.

She was confined to bed for days with few attempts made to assuage her weeping. Muzzie and Aunt Teresa listened to her lamentations as she regretted everything. She relived every argument she and Rudy ever had, rued her words, analyzing every possible thing she did wrong. Her agony consumed her and the chateau's halls echoed with the sounds of her sorrow.

George reminded Natacha of Rudy's love expressed in his final cablegram saying surely their love was as true and strong as it ever was before he died. Day by day Natacha was consoled with love and advice; she should not torture herself with regrets for Rudy would not want her to be incapacitated with guilt and grief.

During the last week of his earth-life, Natacha and Rudy reconciled, experiencing their love renewed. Despite, Natacha drifted at best during those first weeks after Rudy's death; eating little, smoking a great deal. George worried as he watched her sinking into her loss and would later recall.

"Natacha was prostrated by the news. Those who fancy this much misunderstood child to be cold and indifferent should have seen her as I saw her then. Her genuine grief proved her great love for Rudy and her remorse at their misunderstandings and mistakes was heart-breaking to see. I am convinced from my closeness to the true facts surrounding these romantic figures and regardless of what others might say, that Rudy was and ever will be the one real love of Natacha Rambova's earth-life.

I was happy that these two children of the limelight had been reconciled by their exchange of cables before death had stepped in. It made the final separation easier and Rudy made the Great-Change with Natacha's cable under his pillow." [53]

Chapter Nine

Rudolph Valentino Intime

The Hudnut chateau, Juan les Pins, early September, 1926.

"One evening, soon after Rudy's last rites had been preformed in Hollywood, we were all sitting on the round glass veranda overlooking the Mediterranean sea, watching a glorious sunset...when H.P.B. suddenly appeared to me and said,
'Tell Natacha to write the story of her life with Rudy and as an additional part to it Rudy will contribute his revelations. Tell her to begin at once and not delay as it will be a work which will accomplish much good.' " [54]

George would not easily convince Natacha to write a book about her life with Rudy because she felt it far too soon. Yet, it would not be long before Natacha changed her mind and it was then the séances with Rudy began.

According to George, Rudy began to speak through him, delivering messages meant for Natacha to share with the world. With Muzzie seeing her daughter's interest in the project piqued, she began organizing the séances and hired a court stenographer to record Rudy's words. As summer turned to fall, the chateau assumed an air of industriousness with Natacha's writing being the focus of her days. Transcripts were typed, carbon copies filed and the business of Natacha's narrative kept her occupied.

During her day, she reclined on the terrace in a chaise lounge with her dogs on her lap to dictate the story of her life with Rudy to the stenographer. Muzzie would often prompt her with questions and add her own contributions. At night, séances were held with the stenographer present to record Rudy speaking through George.

He related details of the process of his death, the constructs of heaven, mentioning deceased people he met and explaining his aspirations to succeed in his transition. Natacha was mesmerized by the accounts and anticipated the séances as if she were to spend time with her lost lover.

While George was delivering Rudy's first revelations, the world reacted to his sudden death by pursuing Natacha for interviews and commentary. She refused to grant reporters audience when they arrived in droves to the chateau and for a while the task of fielding their questions fell to Uncle Dickie.

Although he was initially an atheist and a skeptic concerning all things psychic, by the end of the summer of 1926, his conversion was complete and he became President of the "Legion de Service Spirituelle" in France. He openly professed his belief in George's abilities and acknowledged life after death as a reality admitting he had witnessed evidence of this himself during many séances.

When a letter arrived from George Ullman in New York relaying news of Rudy calling out the name "Jenny" on the way to the hospital, Uncle Dickie calculated the timing in the séance at the chateau when George called out, "Jenny!" He discovered it would have been the exact time Rudy was being transported to the hospital.

Despite Uncle Dickie's conviction of the legitimacy of spiritualism, the tranquility of his restful chateau in Juan les Pins was disrupted during the weeks following Rudy's death. With stenographers and typists racing about, reporters coming and going, Uncle Dickie Hudnut took control. He announced the summer over and suggested it was time for all to return to Manhattan where they could complete their work and leave him to his peace.

With little argument Natacha and George packed up the dogs and the monkey and boarded the train to Paris, then on to Cherbourg where they left for New York aboard the *Homeric*.

Séances with Rudy would be held in Paris and in Natacha's stateroom on the crossing. By the time the ship neared New York Harbor, Natacha made her decision to co-author her book with Rudy

55

by including his séance messages she titled, "Revelations".

The *Homeric* docked in New York on Thanksgiving Day; two months after Rudolph Valentino's death and Natacha and George's arrival prompted a group of reporters to rush them at the end of the gangplank.

Natacha handed them a story by telling them she had just completed writing a book on her life as Rudolph Valentino's wife. Then to their amazement she announced plans to include a section in the book she would title, "Revelations" which were eleven direct transmissions from Rudy in the after-life as revealed to her during séances.

One reporter called out, "Are you saying, Natacha, that Rudy spoke to you from the dead?"

"Yes, I am," she replied.

When one reporter asked her if Rudy had any messages for his girlfriend Pola Negri, Natacha rebuked the reporter saying,

"Of course not, he spoke only of significant things and subjects that mean something." [55]

She then turned the questions over to George who explained to the scribbling reporters how most of the séances were held in France with some aboard the *Homeric* where Valentino told of wondrous displays in heaven including the celebrities he met there. He also related how Rudy reported he attempted to communicate with his friends as they walked past his bier while he rested in repose in Campbell's Funeral Church. [56]

The following day Natacha and George were pressed for more information and they each granted interviews in their respective apartments. George fielding questions in his home at 614 West 152nd Street[57] and Natacha entertaining press in her luxurious living room.

"The former Mrs. Valentino sought to explain revelations of the astral activities of the dead movie idol. None who watched her as she talked in her apartment could doubt her sincerity. She sat as impassive and oriental looking as the picture of a Chinese mandarin in cloak of gold above her red-lacquered fireplace, her long slim fingers met in a pyramid clasped above her heart.

She exclaimed, 'I do not say these things for publicity. I am not using my husband's name for profit. I am his spokesman giving out what he has told me in spirit séances. Rudy still loves me, otherwise he would not send me messages. I am happy and so is he. I am collecting his messages and will publish them. He was always very psychic.

We had our quarrels. It doesn't matter. What matters most to me now is the effect the uncertainty Rudy's death caused among mortals has on him. He is still in the first of the seven astral planes and has told me he often longed to take me with him to places but he is too new yet.

He knows how I love colors and he always has loved the things I love, colors, music, art, beauty. And he speaks of the colors of that world where he now lives in the fullness of his young manhood. He will be forever young in that world. Ours is but a poor duplicate of it." [58]

While Natacha's news of Rudolph Valentino's "Revelations" rolled off the presses, she spent one chilly November afternoon making final edits on her book while reclined on one of her black velvet sofas. George stands before the great terrace doors as Natacha sorts a few sheets of the manuscript.

"Here, George, this is the end of it," she hands him the papers, "Can you read it for me aloud?"

George takes the pages, "Yes, of course. This is how you want to end the book?"

"Yes, my last word on the subject."

George gives the papers a quick shuffle.

Natacha nods, "Read!"

George clears his throat and begins his read of the end of Natacha's book.

"Both Rudy and I were dreamers and too artistically ambitious. He was as great a worshiper at the shrine of beauty as was I. We both took for our model Douglas Fairbanks, whose great business ability and commercial fearlessness forms a combination difficult to equal.

No, my fault was not selfish ambition; but it was conceit. I was conceited enough to imagine that I could force the producers into giving Rudy the kind of production which our artistic ambitions called for; productions such as *Robin Hood, The Thief of Bagdad* or

The Black Pirate.

I could not understand why with his ability, romance, magnetism and proven drawing power, Rudy should not have the best. Why should he continually be thrust into small, trifling, cheap, commercial pictures while other artists of much less ability and popularity were given big stories and big productions?

The injustice of it made me furious and I stubbornly made up my mind that he should not be so used.

Why should Rudy always be a pawn in the hand of the great iron-fisted soulless god of commercialism? But that same great god only laughed at my puny efforts and clenched his iron fist all the tighter.

It was my passionate love of history and beauty which caused all of the trouble, as do all things carried to unreasonable extremes.

In my intense desire to incorporate beauty into Rudy's productions I lost my perspective. I lost sight of the fact that if beauty is only used as a shallow satisfaction for the eye and not combined with food for the soul as well; it is but an empty gilded shell.

This I have learned. The public will accept a soul-inspiring or touching story which has no outward beauty, but they will not alone accept beauty which has no soul.

The molehill of petty 'hen-pecking' jibes soon grew to proportions of formidable mountain, helped, you may depend upon it, by our many 'friends' who lost no opportunity in showing Rudy any articles of the above description. It was also extremely disagreeable for Rudy to be continually pitied for having a wife who would sacrifice his career for her own selfish ambitions.

Another sore point, it seemed, was the fact that we did not go out often in the evenings or attend the usual Hollywood functions. This was accordingly taken as another proof of my managing; I was jealous, of course and afraid to allow Rudy to be out with other women!

Rudy's friends insisted that he must reinstate himself in the eyes of Hollywood and I was the cause of his being wrongly labeled 'upstage'. He must show Hollywood and the world that he was a regular fellow!

Gloria Swanson was no fool when she packed her belongings and moved to New York, establishing her permanent home in the East; the East where there are at least plays, operas, concerts and museums as diversions from the continual grind.

We started to go out oftener. We did the expected thing. We joined in the 'fun'. We danced, we gossiped, we giggled, we flirted, we laughed, we drank and succeeded in being exceedingly bored.

We even went on 'those amusing expeditions' to Venice (the Coney Island of Hollywood) where we ate 'hot-dogs', rode on the merry-go-round and pretended we were having a hilarious time.

Hollywood! With all the joys of the petty community life of 'Main Street' with an additional coating of gold dust thrown in for good measure.

I am not going to describe any of the widely heralded Hollywood parties with unmentionable details, nor am I insinuating that Hollywood is a 'wicked city' as it is not even that. It is merely an imitation gilded hell of a make-believe realm. Nothing but sham, sham and more sham.

Hollywood, (in speaking of Hollywood, I am referring only to the picture colony) is one continuous struggle of nobodies trying to become somebodies, all pretending to be what they are not.

...It has been said that this earth life is the schoolroom in which we learn our lessons. In Hollywood, like many others, I was given a test and like many others I failed in it. We are also told that we learn our lessons by bitter experience. I think the next time I shall past the test. Rudy is more fortunate, he has already passed onto a higher grade." [59]

George turns to Natacha, "So this is your ending?"

"Yes, of *my* narrative, George." Natacha adds, "But this is followed by Rudy's words, his 'Revelations'."

"Then it shall be, the book is done!" George hands the papers back to Natacha.

"Yes, now Rudy speaks."

George nods as his eye catches a glimpse of frost crackling on one of the terrace door's panes of glass; a small, perfectly formed dragon is taking shape in the rime.

"George?" Natacha asks.

"Yes, what is it?"

"Can you close the drapery?"

George gathers the vermilion velvet saying, "Then the book ends with Rudy's "Revelations"? Wonderful, Natacha, just brilliant!"

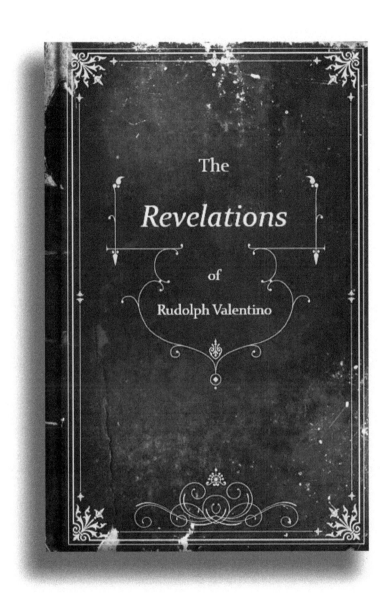

The

Revelations

of

Rudolph Valentino

Rudolph Valentino's *First Revelation* from the Astral Plane

Delivered in the Hudnut chateau in Juan les Pins, September 1926.

I want to tell you how I first met the Great Spirit...

...who has helped me to find myself in these new surroundings and who is teaching me to understand the realities of being; the great spirit of H.P.B. (Helena Petrovna Blavatsky). Rushing back and forth from New York to you, right after my passing, as I did in some unaccountable subconscious way, I found the means of reaching you through George, this channel, this medium, or whatever you may call him. He must have brought me to the particular attention of this teacher, H.P.B.

It was during the time they were taking my body to the west. I was just beginning to feel the loosening of the public's thought which had been centered upon me,

and in a way, I believe, holding me close to the earth. But as newspaper notoriety began to die down and my remains were being piloted to their earthly resting place, I began to feel more alone. The moment the flattering effect of the public's attention was removed, I realized how separated from all these people I was, so far as sight and sound were concerned.

I felt very wretched and lonely. As you well know, Natacha, I have always been easily touched by praise and flattery. The struggles I had gone through and the obstacles I had overcome made the pleasures of public attention all the greater.

But now I stood alone.

There was no one to praise me. I began to feel bitter that I had been cut off in the very height of my activity. I'm afraid I valued myself pretty highly for I could not see how things could go on without me. I can laugh about it now but it seemed a real misfortune to me then.

There was no one to talk to about it and I wandered up and down Broadway. It seemed just as real to me then as it had before. But no one took any notice of me. I could hardly comprehend that they could not see me. I was so real and they were so real that it made the realization of my change very difficult.

I grew tired of dodging out of the way of hurrying people who seemed determined to run into me.

Once I jolted against a woman who headed straight into me and she shuddered and grasped her companion's arm saying, "My what a cold wind just struck me!"

This made me furious. So death had turned me into a cold wind! I would not have it so. I rushed up to a group of actors on the corner of Forty-Seventh Street and Broadway near the Palace Theater. I seized one of the men by the arm and shouted, "I am Rudolph Valentino!" But he paid no attention and went on laughing and talking.

I felt so helpless and useless and yes I felt dead too. At that moment I did not believe in God. For how could God, who let me succeed in my earth life, be so unjust as to let me fail now?

The injustice of it drove me nearly frantic.

Something was very wrong. Here I was, perfectly strong and well only having stepped out of my physical body; not dead but full of force and life. I was standing right on the very corner I had stood on hundreds of times before and yet not a soul could understand that I was there. Natacha, I do not believe I ever have loved people or yearned for their companionship so much as at that moment.

Life seemed so preposterous. It was incredible to me that I, who had been so admired before, was now so absolutely shut out. Oh, I tell you, life seemed cruel.

And then it dawned upon me that I was wrong. These people did not mean to be cruel. They were just as warm-hearted and friendly as I. But they did not know. They had never been told the truth. They were only acting in accordance with the way in which they had been taught.

Then I realized that fault was not theirs. Whose was it? Their parents? Was it the fault of society at large? No, that was not it. At last the idea struck me; who taught society the truths of life? The churches!

They were the ones that were at fault. What was the matter with them? With all of their preaching about the rewards of the next life and eternal salvation and all of the rest of it, of what avail was it if it left me standing there on Broadway being refused recognition? I felt anything but kindly towards the churches. Here I was, dead to the world and all because the churches had inbred in people's minds the false idea that spirits cannot reach back through the veil.

My own church, the Roman Catholic; it understood these facts. The priest who gave me the last sacraments knew it would give my soul a peaceful passing. It did. But what sacrament could continue to give you peace when you frantically banged on the doors of people's consciousness and yet not a single door would open? I tell you Natacha, it is all wrong.

There will never be real peace and happiness on earth until the truth of life and life-everlasting is made clear to people. The churches have not been able to wipe out crime and injustice. But the truths of life and life's positive and active continuance will wipe them out. For people will then understand why they were led to do wrong; they will realize the utter futility of wrong. They will see how useless it is to fool themselves and other people. For spirit sees all!

Oh! the thoughts that coursed through my consciousness as I stood on that street corner. I wept with grief and raged with indignation. But all to no avail.

Then suddenly I thought of you...

...and of the cablegrams you sent me while I lay so ill. I thought of Muzzie's and Uncle Dickie's messages and suddenly someone touched me by the arm.

I turned and looked. A heavily-built woman with kind eyes was standing beside me. I shall never forget her voice, so low and so reassuring, but the vehemency of her language nearly bowled me over.

"Hell, fire and damnation," she said, "so this is how the churches have knocked the wind out of you! Come, there is nothing the matter with the dear old churches except that they are bat-blind. What you need is a friend. I'll be it! I am H.P.B."

Natacha, I didn't know what to say I was so surprised. And the initials H.P.B. meant nothing to me. I did not remember ever having heard them before.

But this strange being only laughed and said, "Come!" I lost consciousness, for how long I did not know, but suddenly I awoke and found myself standing in the big stone hall of Uncle Dickie's chateau. It was night and the big chandelier on the stairs was lit. H.P.B. stood at the top of the stairs and beckoned.

I went up where so often I had gone in my earth life. She led me into Muzzie's room. And there I saw you and Muzzie sitting, George was sleeping, as I thought in a big, easy chair.

"He is in a trance," said H.P.B.,

65

"Now you will be able to speak to your loved ones."

That, Natacha dearest, is how I first came to communicate with you. And that is how I came into contact with H.P.B.

Some time after this she talked to me about reincarnation and theosophy. She laughed and said she would enjoy seeing certain theosophists turn up their noses at the idea of her bothering with the ghost of a dead motion picture actor. But she added, "If theosophy does not teach love and assistance to every living thing in creation, what in thundering blazes does it teach?" This sounded pretty sensible to me and I said so. But of course, I do not know much about theosophy or theosophists. When I asked H.P.B. what theosophy meant, she said, "Theosophy is life and how to live it!" That silenced me pretty thoroughly, for it seemed like a rather large order.

The force in weakening. I must leave. Coming again soon. Good night.

The Second Revelation

Received in Juan les Pins, September 1926.

I Can Not Now View Things in the Same Old Way.

Rushing to you after my passing and finding this means of reaching you through George brought me, as I have told you, to the attention of H.P.B. as all seem to call her.

What a woman! I, at first I was afraid of her. The light, the radiance, I suppose I should call it, almost blinded me. Her eyes made me uncomfortable. They seemed to search out my worst points. And all this happened right in Muzzie's room where you were sitting.

George in a trance and I, with others waiting my turn to speak. H.P.B. stared at me so hard and her light grew so dazzling; whitish gold.

It seemed that I became embarrassed and was about to turn away when a flash of beautiful green, I think ray would be a better word, a ray of clear bright green shot from her towards me and I heard her voice, very soft and low, calling me "Rudy" and "Little Brother".

Somehow all embarrassment left me and I went at once to her. She put her arms around me and said, "Well child, you have left that", and pointed to the walls of Muzzie's room. A change seemed to have come to my sight. For I saw that the walls, the ceiling, the floor and the furniture all gave off a kind of light; but a light that was drab and dull, a sort of putty-grey and brown.

I was able to see straight through the walls of the chateau and to look out into the night. The night did not seem so dark to me as it used to when I was still in my body. It seemed filled with a luminous glow that somehow lit up between the particles of darkness.

This is difficult to express to you. I can hardly find words to describe the new sights and sensations. I could see the trees and the terraces and the Mediterranean beyond. All of these things gave off their own kind of light, but so dull and pale in color.

You know how much I have always loved bright colors. You used to say it was the Italian blood in me.

This strange dullness puzzled me. H.P.B. must have read my mind for she said, "You are seeing the dullness of the earth plane and the pale reflection of loftier and more brilliant spheres." All fear left me.

I began to love this strange woman. Suddenly as I looked at her I saw she became double or sort of turned into two personalities, maybe that is the not the way to express it. But at any rate she appeared in two bodies at the same time. One stood a little behind the other. The one I had seen first was young-looking and very beautiful; so beautiful as to be awe-inspiring. The other was a huge, bulky form, dressed in a shawl and a red petticoat, with a scarf over the head, showing her hair which looked rather crinkly. But the eyes were the same in both; brilliant, piercing and yet very kind.

She must have read my mind again...

...for I was amazed. The beautiful, slender, young figure turned and pointed to the bulky, aged one and her voice said, "That is the H.P.B. that the earth people remember. But I am the H.P.B. of now."

Then behind the bulky form appeared many forms, a long line with one behind the other and yet seeming to dove-tail or merge with each other in an inexplicable way.

H.P.B. laughed and spoke. "Those are my former selves. A damned lot of trouble they have made for me too. But now they are all chained together and come and go as I order them. Like this!"

She waved her arm in a sweeping gesture and instantly all these forms were swept into - what shall I say - well out of sight.

The one that had stood right back of the bulky form had been a man, dark-skinned like a Hindu. "Da! da!" (Yes, yes!) she said, turning in a kind of flash upon me. "That was the shell of the body of the man through which my spirit expressed itself before I came to earth as the Old Lady".

Ever since that time, Natacha, that meeting with Muzzie, you and George; H.P.B. has helped me. Sometimes she has sworn at me soundly and I have been alarmed that perhaps she would leave me. But always at the end of her scolding her smile has reassured me.

After seeing her former selves appear and disappear in this fascinating manner, I was anxious to see my own former selves and asked her how to do it. But I was nearly knocked over by the gale of words she launched at me, "stupid", "fool", "blind pig", and other choice things and winding up by saying, "Poor ignorant darling, can a baby run and leap before it has learned to creep and walk?" So that finished me on that subject for some time to come.

...that it is confusing at times. I have to let go it seems of the old way of looking at things. In the earth world, I, or we, I think I had better say, look only at the outward appearance of people and things and events. We can't help that because we only see the outside. But here we see the outside and the inside as well.

It is really very interesting for the inside lying within the outer shell is always more bright and more active than the outside. It makes me think of the hidden fires of Vesuvius. In this way when I now look at earth people, I see through the body and surface personality and look right at the real self inside. Sometimes this is duller even more than the body. Again, it is more brilliant and beautiful.

The visual aspect of things I have learned and believe I understand pretty well, but the interpretation of them is still something beyond my grasp. But I will learn. H.P.B. says so. And you know Natacha, that I always did accomplish what I set out to do, even if it did take some time.

It is strange but since I am in this new plane of life I do not feel hurried or rushed anymore. I used to always feel when I wanted to do anything that I had to hurry up and that there might not be time enough. But here it is different. Here, I seem to know somehow that there will be time enough and that all I need to do is to go steadily ahead.

Once in a while when I am with you or Muzzie, I feel a little anxious over the results. Then the voice of H.P.B. calls down to me from somewhere, "Steady, darling! Steady!" Her voice often sounds close to my ear even when my eyes do not see her nor my senses feel her presence.

Where is she that she is able to know what I am doing and to answer my thoughts when she is invisible? Another thing for me to learn in time.

This invisible guidance does not frighten me now. You remember the impressions I used to get so often? The thoughts that people were thinking of me? And how it used to startle me? But no more. The most unusual occurrences now seem perfectly usual. The weirdest happenings now seem natural.

So much love I have never seen before. Everyone seems to beam with it. Caruso, whom as you remember I always admired so, comes to me or I go to him. When I asked him about it, he laughed and said, "Well, mio figlio, what does it matter? Are we not together?"

He does not look just as he used to either. He looks more like his music sounded, if you can imagine what I mean. You see, there do not seem to be the right kind of words to tell these things with understanding. But I am doing the best I can and trust to your own keen insight. You used to get thoughts quickly. I hope you do now.

Natacha, they don't know what they are talking about. They are so cramped up in their little bodies, so wound up in their own ideas of self-sufficiency, so looking down. How different the real truth is.

Why don't the churches tell us the truth? Why don't the Jesuit fathers explain the loveliness of life? They know all about it, but they seem to be afraid to come right out with it.

I have such a wonderful sense of freedom now. And no fear. I feel as if I could accomplish anything if I could just know how to go about it. Well, of course, people on earth feel that way too, but there they always have the sense of great obstacles. I know I only have to be shown the way and then start out to accomplish it. On account of this I am sure I will be able to do good work in a while. If I learned to be a good actor when on earth, why can't I be a good helper after I learn? I will.

I do not walk up and down Broadway anymore. There is no use in it. Nobody knows I am there. And it is too dull for me to be happier there.

I sometimes find myself in theaters where my pictures are still being shown. But somehow they do not seem as real to me as they used to. I do not feel so stirred when an audience is moved by my acting or the acting of others. Something about the earth is growing fainter. The world seems to be fading out of my life picture.

People who have not in some way been close to me, or have not really loved me, are now blurred and dim and indistinct to my consciousness. And still I love the earth and its people. I think my ties with the earth are gradually being severed.

I cannot hold the force any longer. Good night, Natacha dear. Do not forget me. Give my love to Muzzie, Uncle Dickie and Aunt Teresa. I feel that all will be well with Aunt Teresa. She was like Gabriella, my own dear mother, and if she comforted me so why should I not provide for her earthly comfort?

Who has the right to change my mind after I have gone? I did what I did with my earthly earnings as I felt to be the fairest way. Alberto, Maria and Auntie were the nearest to me then. They were my little family. Why should they not share and share alike? I hope God will let my way be seen to be the fair way. Good night. I shall come again.

70

The Third Revelation

Juan les Pins, September 1926.

While I was very ill...

...but before it was known for certain that I was to pass over, I suddenly saw, "Jenny". I was so surprised that I think I called out her name. It was only for a moment that I saw her. She stood before me in a glow of rose-colored light. She looked at me and smiled; just as she used to in her earth days when she knew I needed encouragement. She held out her arms.

Her smile seemed to voice the idea, "Do not worry." I did not hear her speak and this vision was all over in a second. But I knew then, Natacha, that I was to go. Deep inside I felt my earthly days to be over. It frightened me. I did not want to go. I had a strange sensation as of sinking out of everything.

The world seemed dearer and brighter than ever it had before. I thought of my work and how I loved it. I thought of my home, of my things and of my pets. Rapidly one thought after another rushed in a tumult in my brain. The thought of cars, travel, yachts, clothes and money. All these material things seemed doubly valuable to me now.

The feeling that suddenly these things were about to be swept away from me or I away from them appalled me. My body screamed deadly heavy and at the same time something within me felt very light as if I was about to be lifted.

Time began to seem very important. Something unknown seemed looming up before me. There was a dreadful sense of immensity all around me which startled my very soul.

I began to think of hundreds of things I had intended to do, important things, trivial things. Even letters that I had intended to write swept across my mind. But the fleeting, though intensely clear vision of Jenny had in some way pushed the power to accomplish these desires far, far away from me. Her strange, beautiful smile, her outstretched arms and the unearthly light around her haunted me.

All this time there was a rumbling sound around me and a jolting sensation as of a moving vehicle. I am not sure, but it seemed to me that I heard George Ullman's voice. Dear, George Ullman!

The thought of people crowded into my mind. Faces, faces, faces! Faces of those I had seen but a few days before and the faces of people I had known long ago in the past. I thought of my fellow cheery workers, of people that relied upon me for help, people of all sorts that ran after me for one thing or another.

Maria's face, Alberto's, Ada's, Aunt Teresa's, Schenck's, Muzzie's and yours! Many, many memories of my father and my mother.

Childhood, Italy, school. My first journey to America and my first papers of citizenship. The rush of thoughts drowned my pain.

Even the most ridiculous experiences, yet all so vivid surged through my memory. Follies, pleasures, griefs; everything I had ever done seemed to come from somewhere and arise to the surface. It made me dizzy. I lost consciousness.

When I came to, the operation had been performed. Everybody smiled encouragingly at me. I had to keep quiet although I felt as if I had so much to say; so much!

But all through these last days, although at times I felt stronger, a weight of dread lay on my heart. I felt that if I could only get up and begin doing many things I had neglected I might lose this dread. Of course they would not let me get up. Your message was near and comforted me.

I had a remarkable feeling that I might see you soon...

...that at any moment you might walk into the room. H.P.B. has since told me that this was because I was soon to go to you instead.

Then I had difficulty breathing and I knew that all was drawing to an end. I was dreadfully frightened. It was too sudden for me to understand it. I don't believe I was actually afraid to die, Natacha; I began to know then that I was changing. I could feel it taking place in my body and my mind. Something seemed to be dropping away. There was at times a straining sensation, as if some part of my

being were tearing itself loose.

I thought of what would happen to my body afterwards; funeral, cremation and the ground. This gave me a sense of horror.

Then the priest came. He seemed like a light in the dark. I turned to him with all my fear, my horror and my uncertainty. My childhood again emerged. Dim cathedral aisles swam before my eyes, the last sacrament!

After the simple ceremony was over, I felt already away from the earth. My mental attitude was changed. The church, like a strong and friendly hand was holding me. I would not be alone. Fear left me. Faces around me grew dim. Silence. Darkness. Unconsciousness.

I do not know how long this lasted. Just as if awakening from a long, deep sleep, I opened my eyes, experiencing at the same moment a feeling as of being rapidly drawn upward; then wonderful bluish light, then Black Feather, Jenny and Gabriella, my mother! I was dead. I was alive. This, Natacha, is the remembrance of my passing.

The Fourth Revelation

Juan les Pins, September 1926.

Because I knew something about life after death...

...before I came over, it has not taken me long to find myself. That is, to acclimate myself to these new conditions. My automatic writings that you enjoyed so much, Natacha, taught us a great deal. You remember the writings given from the spirits of Jenny, Mesolope, Black Feather, Oscar and many others.

We did not always pay as much attention to them as we should have. It was just so interesting to find them interesting. It is difficult to put real help and advice into our daily lives, isn't it?

But since I have come over the memory of these writings has served to put me in closer touch with life as it really is and not the false aspect often given out by people who know little to nothing about it. And my natural powers of observation have helped me to progress quicker than if I were slower in that respect.

I find that our powers in the body are about the same but heightened to a considerable degree when we are freed from it. I am now the same old Rudy you knew before, only now I am a Rudy heightened in perceptive facility. And I seem to feel emotions more keenly too. Spirits tell me that this is because I am still in my astral desire body.

The earth body itself does not feel, it is only a material covering or shell for the astral body which does feel. I am so glad to be able to tell you this so that when you have a sort of pain, you will know it is not in your earth body but in your astral body.

Spirits have shown me how easily the astral body can be vitalized by currents of vitality. They say these vitalizing currents are the life emanations of God. When the astral body is cut off from this supply it cries out in pain which is really a warning to you to try to bring it into contact again with the currents of healing.

When this is done the cause of

pain is of course removed and the pain ceases. H.P.B. has shown me how this astral body often withdraws itself from the physical body. This happens to people who are in deep sleep.

At night I have seen your astral body emerge...

...from your physical body and I have been able to get very close to your consciousness and talk to you. You have sometimes remembered this vaguely upon awakening and thought it only to be a dream. But it was no dream. It was the living reality.

When George goes into a trance, his astral body comes out. In the earth life when this happens, the astral body is connected to the physical body by a shining cord which seems to be attached to the head. I do not yet understand just how this is but this is what I have myself seen.

Spirits have also told me that when anesthetic is given the astral body emerges and that is why there is no longer any sensation left in the physical body. This is all interesting to me. When people on earth are able to heal others by putting their hands upon them, it is because they are simply allowing the vital currents to flow through them into the devitalized body of a part.

I learned a lot of this at some lectures I attended, Natacha. You would love the lectures here. There are places they call "centres". To me they look like temples. They are white and very lofty and beautiful. I thought they were of stone but the spirit of George's guide, Henry Watts, told me they were constructed of the white thought-force of truth and faith.

Everything seems to be made of one or another kind of thought-force. The thought-substance it seems, is far more solid and enduring than the stones or metals of the earth world. This is hard to realize. It does not look at all as one would suppose thought-force ought to look. I always imagined it to be a misty, cloud-like sort of thing and here it is more solid and colorful than the solid objects on earth. Life is truly amazing and I love it more and more.

I have seen some amazing houses here. Some like little villas and others much more imposing and magnificent. These, it seems, belong to people who were quite humble in the earth life, even poor. But they were people who had not denied shelter to those who needed it. They had divided their meals with those who were hungry. And on account of their generosity they have found these places built for them out of the thought-substance of their actions.

It seems very thrilling to me...

...and I could not keep back the tears when I realized how this was done. The houses are built by the spirits who have learned to mold this thought-force. They are always built just as the people to live in them would like to have them. The spirit builders know how to do this by looking into people's unconsciousness where, it seems, the mental pictures of all they love and desire are stored.

Some of the houses are only partly built as enough thought-substance has not yet been sent over from unselfish actions. There are also large places like various kinds of hotels, where people who have no such homes are kept for a while. These are the selfish, uncharitable ones who have not shared. These are the people who have denied assistance to those who are in need.

I knew lots of people like that and now I am sorry for them. These people are talked to but not in a preachy sort of way and are taken to see plays showing up such subjects.

There is even a way of showing them picture-like flashes of their own past actions. This is the nearest thing to a motion picture that I have seen. But it is not like that. It is all done by thought processes. H.P.B. says it is the instructive incidents in a soul's past brought forward and out of the astral light.

This is all done in the hope that people will realize their mistakes and start to change their attitudes of thought. If they do desire to change, work is at once given to them. There is plenty of work everywhere. They are given what they are most adapted to. In that way they lose sight of self in seeing others being helped and so begin to form the thought-substance that will build their homes.

If they do not desire to change but hang on to their old ideas stubbornly, they are turned out to wander alone. No one feels at all sorry for them. This surprised me very much at first. But how can you change their minds to begin to earn all they desire? They are fools to say the least.

I am told they do not wander around very long. The supreme indifference by which they are met soon brings them to their senses. I have seen some very beautiful houses that belong to people who were wealthy on earth. But they were people who never failed to help others. They shared. They realized what their wealth was for.

At first when I heard about all of this I began to think it was wrong to try to get rich in earth life. But H.P.B. tells me this is not so. She says it is right for people to be rich if they do good with their riches. She says they have at some time earned the right to possess those riches and they are being tested. What they possess in the future seems to depend upon what use they make of what they possess in the present.

Learn these truths now Natacha dear, and teach them to your friends. Do not wait until the time of your coming over here.

H.P.B. says it is not true generosity to give recklessly however. Thought and common sense must be used always. Only the really needy should be reached. And not too much help should be given at once. This would make weak people weaker. The best help she says, is the kind that helps people help themselves. In that way they grow stronger and more reliant.

I asked her about impostors. You know Natacha how often I was approached by them. H.P.B.'s answer was, 'If I had not the vision to distinguish true from false, I would rather give aid to an impostor than lose the chance of helping one who might really be needy."

Henry Watts says that all souls need some kind of help. We must share whatever we have whether it be possessions or knowledge. So this is what makes that thought-force substance of which homes are built. I wish I had known this in my earth life. I would have done many things differently. But you can depend on it now that I am going to try to put what I learn into action. I want to progress.

I would like to become a guide. But friends of my profession whom I have met here tell me I had better stick to the theater.

It turns out that the unusual magnetism I possessed when appearing on the screen was due to the fact that I have been an actor in previous lives.

I wish I knew what those lives were and who I was. I am told that an account of all one's experiences are indelibly stamped on the Great Records and can be reviewed in the Astral Light. But one cannot do this until one has learned how or earned the right. This is another thing I am anxious to learn. You see, there are a good many things that make life fascinating.

My friends have taken me to see the theaters. They are enormous and very beautiful. They are also built of thought-substance but of that thought-substance which comes from true poet's ideals. You cannot imagine how wondrous in form and color these theaters are.

In these theaters many thousands of spectators are enabled to watch the performances. The plays are great dramas of the soul. For these theaters the writers create for the joy of creating and not for the need of money. So of course marvelous plays are to be seen.

All the great actors act in them. But there is a strange difference in the acting here and the acting of earth. On the earth plane a clever artist can portray any part given to him by a manager. Not so here. There is more cleverness here. All is sincerity.

No artist can portray a single emotion that his soul is not capable of expressing in reality. There is no

77

imitation. There is no assuming and all is real. All is genuine and true.

An actress can not play a role of noble quality unless she has truly developed that noble quality in her own soul. There is no sham here. A man cannot portray a king unless he is majestic in character or soul. On earth the Passion Play comes nearest to this sincere expression.

Artists are not allowed to play evil roles...

...unless the evil to be portrayed has been overcome by artists themselves in some former life experience. Evil is only portrayed to serve a purpose and to heighten the effect of the good.

There is no scenery on the stage in the sense that there is scenery in the earth world theaters. The mood and purpose of the play create a thought-substance reflecting it and this substance, colored accordingly, forms a great and perfectly natural background for the performance.

And the actors, according to the emotions being expressed give off thought-forms, brilliant or somber, according to the particular emotion. These thought-forms, playing against the background of the mood form a marvelous symphony of color.

No words are actually spoken as upon earth. The ideas are all expressed in thought. And as ideas are universal, all earth plane languages merge into one in this after-life. So the spectators, no matter what their language on earth might have been, understand fluently the thought language of the drama.

Oh Natacha, I know you would love it.

Yes, I feel I do belong to the theater and I shall be so happy when they let me begin to play, even if the parts they give me at first are small. I am told there is no jealousy among the artists as there is in the earth world. There cannot be. Everyone knows he can only play what he is fitted for by soul experience to play. Here, no one can step in and play another's part, for there are no two emotions alike. Life is too many sided for that. All work together in harmony, intent upon the purpose of the drama and of the service it will give to the spectators.

The force is gone. I cannot communicate any longer. I have more to say on this and will continue another time.

The Fifth Revelation

Juan les Pins, September 1926.

I have been taken to hear some wonderful operas.
You remember how much I loved music. The operas are not given in theaters as in the earth-plane but in immense and very wonderful temples. Music here is sacred and is always listened to in reverence. Do not let this alarm you, Natacha. When you hear the kind of music it is you will understand. You have no music like it on the earth-world.

I would not be able to tell you all about this if it were not for the fact that Caruso explained it to me. It is he who took me to listen to the opera. He also took me all over the temple. Caruso sings here very often as do all the many singers who have come over.

Enrico says that the great composers here know that life itself is music. They have learned to strike the keynote of many vibrations. Of course they have not mastered them all but they are constantly studying to do so. Since everything is vibration you can see what a study it is.

In this way, Caruso says, real and true music is created. Music that mirrors every emotion the human entity is capable of expressing. Also the multitudinous sounds of the natural world and the unearthly music of the planets in motion.

In the earth-plane the number of keys is very limited, there being only twenty-four scales, Caruso says. But here, composers have discovered that the number is unlimited. There are as many keys as there are different vibrations. That is why music is such a vast and inexhaustible subject.

Earth-plane ears could not define those keys of which I speak. Only the inner ear, the psychic ear - the soul's true ear - is fine enough to catch these sounds. But Natacha, music composed in these keys is so exquisitely sublime that it lifts the listening soul to the very heights of ecstasy. Caruso says that if earth - plane ears could hear it, the intense vibration effect upon the nervous stem would be so great as to shatter.

79

Music here is not used only to please the senses or to appeal to the intellect; it has far higher purposes. H.P.B. says it is the idealized soul of vibration and therefore has unlimited power for good or bad, depending upon how it is directed.

It is used to harmonize large bodies of people. It is used to key them to a higher pitch so that in this way they are lifted to a higher plane temporarily for purposes of instruction. Certain planets are also communicated with by means of this kind of music.

I asked H.P.B. about this and she explained it, but I do not think I can give it to you as clearly as she did to me. But it seems that each planet has its particular keynote or scale and that everything on that planet has a keynote that is in relationship with the main scale. I hope I am saying this so you will understand. My language may not be technical enough but I am doing my best.

The music by which the North Star is reached...

...is peculiarly magnetic in attractive quality and rather metallic in tone. There are planetary spirits you know and H.P.B. says those of the North Star are adepts in guidance. That is why in the earth-world it has been used as a focus point for adventurous travelers from time immemorial. All compasses point toward it. She says if people who are confused and lost on their way, as it were, would only collect themselves and become calm enough to turn to the spirits of the North Star, their confusion would cease and they would find guidance. Whenever you lose your way Natacha, in the mazes of life, turn to find the right direction from the vibrations of the North Star. She calls this star Isis. It affects other worlds than the earth-world.

The music of Venus is glowing and vibrant with vital force, says H.P.B. I can't remember what she said about Mercury, but the music of Saturn and Uranus was described as exotic and hypnotic and could be used for evil if people knew how.

Neptune's music, she said, is so peculiar that earth-people would never comprehend it. It would sound to them either like a thunderous roar or else like a faint twinkling of a wavelet against a wavelet.

The music of the Moon is calm, but compelling. It acts, she says, mesmerically upon all fluids. Composers who are able to tap inspiration from the Moon vibration are always able to sway and win their listeners by their creations. Such inspiration is hauntingly beautiful, yet strangely pale and metallic in coloring.

The Sun music as H.P.B. explained it; well, here are her words,"a drenching dew of heaven's melody, life-giving, sustaining, creating." It is the music of eternal creation, of joy unlimited. Every soul echoes it, she says, but earth-souls are deafened by its tremendous harmonies and do not realize that it is the symphony of their life.

There are other planets, the music of which she described, but I could not retain all this learning at one time. The greatest of all planetary music, she said emphatically, was that of Isis, the magnetic Star of the North.

Guardian spirits of certain souls in the earth-world often use music to quell storms and to avert disasters when it does not interfere with Karmic Laws. You know there are stories and legends of sailors hearing strange music in the midst of storms and of the waters being mysteriously calmed. These stories are all founded on psychic facts.

Certain healings are also affected by it. Florence Nightingale, the well-remembered nurse of your world, told me this. She says that very often patients lying near death's door hear, as in a dream, glorious voices, or ethereal music, and are soon after restored to health and after-life. And how often, she says, does the departing soul hear this wondrous music of the spheres as it leaves the body and is received beyond the veil?

Oh, Natacha, cara mia...

...that veil is not away, nor is it so thick as earth-people like to believe.

The operas are given as dramas here. Only the scenic display of color is far greater. You, with your earthly conceptions cannot begin to conceive the intricate beauty and glory of this color play. Music seems to show itself in colors more vivid and more piercingly bright than do the thought-forms.

Not long ago - I think that is how to say it, for I seem to have lost track of time here - I heard Caruso in an opera called *The Journey of the Soul.* When I say I heard Caruso in it I say so because he seems nearer to me than others. But I heard many great singers in it. There were great choruses visible and invisible. At one time the music rose to such a height of grandeur that other planes were contacted and we heard the answering choruses from those planes.

This is one of the most remarkable things I have learned about music here - how it does not seem to be just a finished thing of itself as an opera in the earth-world is. Here, music links with other music in other planes. Of course, I cannot begin to understand how or why this is but it is so.

Natacha, I have never heard anything like this opera in all my experience; you see I do not say "in all my life" anymore. My whole soul wept for joy. Caruso's voice soared out to us like the tones of some great organ and the colors that poured from his aura while he sang were infinite in variety - brilliant shades of gold and many tones of violet and purple.

There were flashes of silver too at times and a color I have never seen before: a kind of color between silver and copper, with a pale green such as you see in certain metals mixed in with it. There are so many colors here that we cannot see in

81

the earth-life.

You above all people would be thrilled with all this color. At one time during the opera I suddenly lost all sense of sight or sound or feeling. The prismatic display disappeared, I no longer heard the music and I was no longer swayed by the emotion. I became frightened and turned to H.P.B. who sat beside me.

She laughed and said, "Little fool, it is simply that your soul has not progressed enough yet to be able to comprehend this part of the opera. These colors are beyond your present powers of visualization. This music is in too high a rate of vibration for your soul to feel. Have patience. Learn to wait and grow."

Wasn't that curious? What would I do without H.P.B.? There must be something good in me to have attracted her as a helper. I always seem to be able to understand her words and they are indelibly stamped on my memory. I do not forget the things she says.

This is all I can tell you about music for it is all I have learned. I am so anxious to study and learn. Are you pleased that I am doing so?

Before I leave I want to tell you that after the opera I was so excited, I wanted to bring you in your astral body while you slept, to experience one too. I asked the spirit of Henry Watts about it but he said I must not attempt it. To do so took great experience and of course I am so new here yet. He said if I tried I might do you great harm.

But all the same I wish you could hear and see one. It is really worth dying just to experience this indescribable beauty. I still love beauty just as much as I did on earth.

Buena notte, for the present. I will come again soon. I feel so happy, so fortunate to be able to reach you again and you, carissima, know why.

The Sixth Revelation

Juan les Pins, October 1926.

It seems so strange to me now...

...as I look back on my earth-life, how blind to realities we are on the verge of truths and yet in our blindness pass them by. If only our inner vision were more developed. There would then be no misunderstandings, ridiculous and foolish as they always are when looked back upon such as yours and mine.

Had we that keener vision, we would see that such petty difficulties are only like winter frost on a window pane. Frost that would melt at the first warm breath of a word of love.

But no. We do not wait to even try to see. We act at once, impetuously and without reason. Our anger, muddy-red and blinding and bewildering, suffices our facilities, clogs our perceptive channels and altogether drags us downward. H.P.B. has explained this so well to me because at first I was quite confused as I looked back upon our differences and our parting.

Now it is all much clearer to me. She says that when this red cloud of anger surges over us it attracts, through appearing in our aura, the attention of destructive entities, both human and elemental. This muddy color is to them an invitation to advance.

They swarm about us and through our consciousness. Their delight in destruction and their intense desire to drag down other souls to their own level, is so great that our anger is intensified. We finally, when we give in to anger repeatedly, fall under their domain entirely. These entities do not let go easily. Their method of victimizing is poisonously patient.

You and I were both head-strong and prone to rapid anger and H.P.B. has shown me how we both attracted destructive forces that ended our earth-plane union disastrously. But now we know this was only frost upon the windows of our souls. The unclouded vision of my spirit has melted that now.

It is so, too, with people I did not like very much when in the earth-life. Now, as I look at them and see beneath their surfaces, I see a great deal in them to love. They would, no doubt, laugh if I told them this but ignorant laughter never changes truth. Does it? It is very easy to scoff. But truth remains truth all the same. If we insist upon learning it in our earthly existence we shall most certainly learn it here. We could not avoid learning it even if we wished as our eyes become clear-seeing and these verities stand out most startling.

Thank Heaven I was always adaptable to my surroundings. This faculty stands me in good stead here. H.P.B. says it is on account of this that I am acquiring knowledge of this plane so rapidly. She says adaptability is a sense of unity and leads eventually to oneness.

This place where I am living is the astral plane. But that term is very expansive. When we used to get automatic messages about it, I always thought it was a realm of rather low spirits.

Now I find that while it does take in those misguided spirits always very close to the earth, it still embraces many progressed souls as well. All these lovely places I have told you of are in it.

It seems to be, as far as I can make out, a place of progression where many problems are worked out. It is a place where souls are awakened to realities. It is a sense of purgatory for the Roman Catholics. I used to worry a good deal about purgatory.

Well here I am in it and I do not find it anything other than interesting. Of course, if I were stubborn and clinging to old desires and prejudices and jealousies and quarrels, I should likely find it a pretty lonely place. There are the lonely ones here, the discouraged ones and the evil ones too. But help, when sought is ever present. How thankful I am to know this!

It is strange how people in the earth-world like to say that communications are possible but only from the ignorant, evil and misguided spirits. Being the nearest to the earth does not in any way make them the nearest to humanity at large. In fact, the guides tell me that it separates them more completely. They are near only to people who attract them and who are somewhere in their natures of like caliber.

But there are exceptions. Under certain conditions these souls are allowed to communicate for purposes of gaining deliverance for themselves. At other times to serve as illustrations to certain lessons the guides are giving.

Natacha dear, if such undeveloped souls are in any manner able to communicate or appear to people of the earth, does it not stand to reason that more advanced souls - souls that were helpers and teachers in the earth-life - would with their keener intelligence, soon find the way to communicate their knowledge of this after-life?

Why am I striving to communicate with you? Because I love you. And I love the people of the earth. If my new learning that I am gaining every minute, hour and day, every atom of time is of profit to you, it may be of profit to others. And so I am making haste to give it to you and to that world.

How fortunate I am to have so trained and facile an instrument to come through. Of course, Natacha, I am helped to do so by several spirits. Sometimes it is Annie, the mother of the medium who assists me to hold myself in the medium's vibration. Sometimes it is Henry Watts, or Ami, or Alestes or U.K.

and often it is H.P.B. herself.

You see it is this way. Being now in the life of the spirit, I am vibrating at a much more rapid rate than when in a physical body. I could come to you, or Muzzie or Uncle Dickie or Aunt Tessie and speak all day and yet you would not hear me. Your vibration is so much slower. And you can sense things in your own vibrations.

But mediums are vastly different. Thank God for the power that lets such peculiar organisms exist! They are so constituted as to possess variable rates of vibrations. When a medium is to be used he is put in working order by special guides who have made a study of this. White Cloud, the old Ojibwa Indian is the guide who does this for George.

Now I will tell you exactly how I communicate with you, Natacha.

You decide to have a séance.

You and Muzzie, Aunt Tessie and Uncle Dickie. You are all seated in your chairs in a circle, George in his easy chair - we call it the receiving station. George relaxes and making his mind a blank (I don't know any better way to express it) leaves the body. His mother takes charge of his soul in his astral body and takes care of the astral cord for it is the connecting link between spirit and matter. His mother is the best one to do this service as she is nearest to him in vibrational key. In a way, it is fortunate for George's psychic work that his mother has passed to the life of the spirit.

White Cloud takes charge

always of the sleeping physical body which is limp and empty now. The body is now vibrating much more rapidly than in normal activity. The blood is drawn magnetically inward around the nerve centers, spinal cord and brain. The body is giving out certain musical sounds; if you could but hear them!

Sometimes there is not enough magnetism in the medium's body to accomplish the entrance of a spirit, so a surplus is drawn from the sitters; from Muzzie, Aunt Tessie, Uncle Dickie and you. Other guides do that. Henry Watts or Ami, or Black Feather. When enough magnetism is obtained we, by

85

means of it, animate it - often clumsily at first - and speak to you as best we can.

At first I could not learn to enter the body very well and could only get in a word or two. That was because I was told to focus my mind upon lowering my vibrations to the rate of the medium's. This is done through sound. The sound I spoke of coming from the medium's body, is the pitch we have to key our vibrations to. We sing in our mind the same tone, as it were. I hope I am making this clear. I am trying the best to do so.

But I found this extremely hard to do. When I started to speak to you I would forget to keep the vibration note in mind and immediately up would go my vibration and I would find myself out of George's body. Then White Cloud would help me to be drawn in again by the attraction to the magnetic current. I could hear you all saying, "Oh, don't go, Rudy. Come back and talk to us!"

You can see that it takes practice to be able to enter a body, stay there and speak clearly and fluently to our loved ones. That is why with many mediums, Henry Watts explains, the messages are sometimes so trifling and incoherent. But George's vibration is unusually steady most of the times and that is why we can control him so long at a time and speak so definitely and clearly through him.

Now about names, Natacha dear. You and others have remarked how often spirits are able to give their names clearly through George's mediumship. And when you went to many other mediums you got very few names. The reason for this, I find, has to do with sound also.

Our given name is the name that belongs to us inherently.

At any rate the name identifies us, whether it was a baptismal name or a name assumed, is the part of the full name that represents us. Now it seems that this name is some way as yet unexplained to me is a power - a vibrational power. And whenever it is thought of or called into being, it sounds its individual keynote.

When during communication we are keeping our mind on the vibrational rate tone, in order to stay in the body and attempt to give our name to you, the keynote of the name sounds. This, confusing with the vibration rate note upsets our concentration and sometimes dislodges us entirely from the body or causes us to mumble or give the name indistinctly. Try it and see. And the moment you let go of the medium's vibration rate tone, which keys you to him, up bobs your own vibration and you have let go of the control.

I am afraid I have repeated a lot in explaining this. But as it appears rather complicated I cannot seem to help it.

With a medium like George, whose vibration is generally so steady, it is much easier to hold the tone as his tone is not so constantly wobbling up and down as in the case of many.

At the beginning when I could control in this way hardly at all, I would give up trying and would tell White Cloud to say things to you for me. Spirits coming to a particular medium for the first time are seldom able to control unless they have had experience in coming through other mediums. The method of control is practically the same with all mediums, I am told. Although I have not tried any number yet.

I am having the time of my life learning all these ways and means. Life-existence is the most fascinating study. I am filled with the joy of it. I have much more to tell you but the force is growing less now and I must let up my control.

I will soon come again.

The Seventh Revelation

Juan les Pins, October 1926.

One thing that pleases me beyond everything...

...is that I find a nature world here, just as in the earth-world. Only here it is more radiant. I think this is the world nearest to what I mean - anyway and far more beautiful. There are plains, mountains, rivers, lakes, trees, flowers and birds.

The trees seem greater in height and their lofty branches are heavier with foliage and of a green far clearer than on earth. The flowers are intensely brilliant. They do not seem composed of the firm petals we are used to in the earth-life. They seem to be instead forms of living color, vibrating or constantly glowing as it were. This is hard for me to describe.

H.P.B. says I am still so new to this change of dimension that I keep comparing things to the old way. These glowing color forms are the souls of the flowers; their bodies left on earth to decompose into mold.

I notice a much clearer and stronger fragrance with these soul flowers. H.P.B. has also told me that the perfume of flowers in the earth-plane consists of the effect of the flowers' auras on your olfactory nerve centers. She says that this fragrance - these various odors - are in themselves color emanations. The mortal eye is not developed enough to see them but the sense of smell catches the vibration. So you see Natacha it all comes back to vibration.

H.P.B. also says that if people's noses were as dull as their eyes, scientists would probably swear up and down that flowers gave forth no odors! She says that every flower gives out some kind of fragrance because souls of any kind whatsoever possess auras. But some of these perfumes are too delicate for even the sense of smell to detect. People therefore claim such flowers to be odorless.

H.P.B. told me that mediumistic eyes often see these perfume vibrations and some people, she explained, are so sensitive that they are able to feel these flowers vibrations.

This idea seems to make sound,

color, taste, feeling and odor to be simply different effects of the same cause; different degrees of vibration. At least that is how I have figured it out so far.

I asked H.P.B. if that didn't reduce life to just different expressions of the same thing. She smiled and said, "Yes, dear child, and that thing is God and God is love and love is expression and expression is creation and creation is truth and truth is nine multiplied by nine indefinitely which reaches back to God again. And so the circle of life is complete." I guess she thinks I ask an awful lot of questions but she always takes the trouble to answer me.

There seems to be every variety of flowers that you have on earth blooming here with many others I have never seen before. The beauty of these astral flowers is beyond my power of description. Many of them are geometric in form and color effect and some are very complicated in structure. There are such quantities of these curious astral flowers, new to me, that I have only learned to know a few of them.

There is a kind whose blossoms twist upward in a spiral, the top cluster ending in a point. These are of every hue that a prism is capable of giving off. They are called, "Flames of the Soul."

Another extremely interesting kind is popularly called, "Heart Beats", but H.P.B. says they are the real "Immortals". They are very delicate and have but one pendant heart shaped blossom of glowing white light. A current of red life force is continuously coursing through the center of the semi-transparent blossom, pulsating like a heart beat.

These flowers are so sensitive...

...in reacting to conditions or vibrations to which they have been keyed that spirits use them as a kind of barometer by which they gauge the health of their earth-friends and the state of affairs around them. It is a most curious plant. I have not seen a house here that does not have them blooming in the garden.

One can see many spirits going earthward carrying these beautiful plants. They take them to earth and leave them for a while in the houses of their loved ones. The "Beating Heart" flowers in some way become tuned to the true keynote of the vibration of the earth personality through absorbing the auric emanation. And they retain this vibrational pitch until the earth death of the person to whose vibrations they have become tuned.

Later, the spirits take back these flowers to their own homes on the astral plane and by noting the pulsation of the red life force within the transparent white flower, can tell exactly the condition of the earth person it is keyed to; whether he is calm or agitated, well or ill and even when he is going to die.

Spirits seem to be very happy when a "Beating Heart" flower

shows them the coming death of a relative or friend. They all get together in a meeting - something like our parties of the earth-world - with singing and dancing. They are all so pleased that another soul is coming into the realness of life.

Do not be surprised that I say there is dancing over here, Everyone dances. But not exactly in the way of the earth. It is mostly symbolic and is the expression in action of one's higher emotions. I can well imagine some of our friends, Natacha, thinking this is rather highbrow, but let me tell you it is not so. The music is so wonderful that everyone is caught by it and just lets go and expresses himself in rhythm. You will enjoy it when you come over because you are a natural dancer.

High souls like to tell you there is no jazz here but that is not quite true. There is. But you have to now where to find it.

Wally Reid [60] has told me all about it and he even took me to see it. You will find this kind of dancing on the lower astral plane. That past of the astral world that dovetails into the earth. So all that sort of thing is quite near to you. I will tell you more about these people at another time.

You will be pleased to hear that I have met Vernon Castle [61] again. He is just the same charming fellow. He told me a good deal about dancing too.

Vernon says that for the people still on the earth dancing is very excellent. He explained to me how dancing sets in motion, within the physical body, currents of nerve force that go spiraling up the spinal cord until they reach two glands in the brain called pituitary and pineal. These glands are great psychic centers.

Vernon told me that the lower forms of dancing are not good and because of their attracting deteriorating entities they hinder the souls' progress. They stir lower desires and allow the wrong kind of elementals (nature spirits) and sensual human spirits to use a hypnotic influence upon the mind. It seems these spirits have a way of merging themselves into the physical bodies they contact by these means and are then able to experience more sensation.

The study of these facts is more fascinating to me and it throws light on many things that puzzled me during my earth-life. I now understand the causes for the actions of certain people I used to meet and whom, I am afraid, I was too ready to condemn.

Now I know why they threw their life chances to the winds - allowing themselves to be controlled by entities through their lower desires - and I am very sorry for them.

Dear, wild Hollywood, the scene of my struggles and my triumphs - what a place it is of undeveloped souls. There are wonderful souls there. There are broken souls there. And there are many souls that might be great were they not being suffocated by the intense materialism of that artificial life.

With the knowledge I now have of life, gained by my clearer

perceptions and the help of my teachers, I would not care to return to the life of Hollywood.

Life there is superficial and a sham and such conditions are not lasting. I always did love out-of-doors and nature and that I think is what sustained me through it all. Over here I find that nature is so very important. People do not realize its importance in their lives.

It is important because it is so closely linked to us to the physical body and at the same time with inner character. Earth bodies are composed of the elements of earth, the same currents of force flow through them and all the beauty that the earth can produce is reflected in our inner character.

Oh, Natacha, I want to tell people to go out among the trees and flowers and birds. Tell your friends to do so. Look up gladly into the blue ether overhead and realize that greater planes of life are there. Then look around at the gloriousness of nature and realize that a great plane lies there. Then try to consider how closely joined together are all these planes, like the links of a beautiful chain. The thought of planes linking together will give you the idea of brotherhood.

Never feel sorry when you see trees falling before the woodcutter's ax. H.P.B. say the nature world gladly serves humanity and by doing so fulfills its mission, destiny or purpose and finds its evolution and advancement. Perhaps I do not know just how to say this.

Of course, ruthless destruction, I am told, is waste and waste is very wrong. Service is quite another matter.

The force is gone. I have more to give another time and will come again.

The Eighth Revelation

Juan les Pins, October 1926.

Here I meet so many wonderful souls. There is no holding aloof and waiting for introductions. Nothing like that. I find life here to be a true brotherhood. Our likes and longings are met with an understanding response.

If I have admired any particular person for his life and work, that person psychically knows of it without any words to that effect and extends immediately the hand of fellowship. So you can see that life in these planes beyond earth is on a truer basis than we have known before.

One's innermost thoughts, I have learned, are revealed to anyone in the same degree of development or higher. For instance, all people here who have attained the soul development that I have and I guess that is very little so far, can read my deepest thoughts. And souls that are more and more advance than I can not only read these thoughts but can see the reason for them and underlying cause of them. In this way, you see, there are no secrets. And by this clear-seeing of others can one alone be helped.

It made me very uncomfortable at first, for we all have a foolish pride about our hidden likes and dislikes becoming known. But when I realized that this reading of the character was a fact, I thought it best to act like a sport and so I gave in at once.

This brought to my surprise a feeling of intense relief. It seemed as if a load had dropped away from me. I felt nearer to the truth than ever before and far nearer to people - real people. I then realized that there was brotherhood and unity and protection.

Life on earth would be vastly different I am sure if people only knew the actual conditions they were going to face sooner or later

92

through death. That is why I am anxious to tell these facts as I discover them.

It is interesting to me to see how people here, that is people who are at all awakened seem bent only upon trying to unfold their latent spiritual qualities. You see, we have all left behind the things of earth; our business, professions, money, property and all our worldly pursuits.

We find ourselves absolutely shut away from all this; that is from continuing in the same old way and discovering ourselves standing ready to begin an entirely new life. With what it seems at first an apparently blank future slate before we pass over, this literally new birth come to us as a very great shock.

Many people cannot hold up...

...against this shock and surprise. So they, through ignorance, fear and resentment at having been taken from the material world they loved too well spend all their time haunting their familiar earthly surroundings and become tied, mentally to the earth. They are in the lower astral plane, out of the world, yet they are still in it through their tenacious clinging to worldly attitudes of thought. These unfortunate people are the earth-bound we used to hear about in automatic writings.

I am told that some of these souls are so stubborn and so anchored down by the set conviction of their former mode of thinking that they are actually blinded and cannot see or realize the possibilities of advancement in the newer world before them. They are unadaptable, obstinate and unprogressive.

They are the ones, who when in the earth-life were the first to oppose innovations of any sort. And you may be surprised to learn that they are in all walks of life. There are among this type of earth-bound, ministers of the gospel, priests and religious men of all kinds who have been hidebound to their creeds, superstitions and beliefs. Among them are many fanatics.

There are also kings and queens and all sorts of people of the ruling classes who will not let go of the ideas of temporal power. There are countless souls too of the humbler classes who are tied by the limited aspect of their thoughts; peasants who still cannot see more than ten feet before their plows, soldiers who insist upon believing their might is right in spite of the fact that death has proved otherwise to them. All who are narrow and pinched in the mental outlook are tied and earth-bound.

The worst of it is; these souls may be bound in this way for years as you count them, even for centuries. To me this is a rather appalling aspect.

The best of it is the very moment such a soul changes his mental attitude, he at once realizes the folly of clinging to limitations.

Then if he has any sense at all, he will let go, turn right about face and so go marching on.

Scientific people of all kinds, I am informed, change their attitudes very readily. They may have been unbending in their views when on earth but for all that they were in their own wonderful way seekers. When the stark realities of a new existence stare them in the face, they are not stupid about it but immediately regard the matter as a new specimen to be inspected through the microscopes.

I must tell you at first I was somewhat held back by my earthly egotism. I can now look back at it and laugh. H.P.B. has shown me how humorous it appeared to such spirits watching me and who tried to help me. I actually thought the motion picture industry would be fatally crippled without me. I imagined I was about the greatest actor on earth. After seeing the acting in theaters over here, I blush in my very soul to think of my conceit.

I was angry too when the helpers confronted me with my egotism. I was angry because I was really ashamed to find out that this was true. I know it even appalled you - my colossal egotism - when I expressed my opinions through the medium at the chateau, upon my highly esteemed self. But Uncle Dick and Arthur Forrest and Mrs. Cora Brown-Potter too, were all wonderful about it. None of them laughed at me. They even agreed with my views of how great an actor I thought I was.

But that is because Arthur and Cora are artists and Uncle Dickie wanted to say the sporting thing. They all knew well enough that there is always someone ready to go right on with any work that is left behind. I know it now, too.

People, people, people! They are what really count. I love them more and more as I come to know them in a spiritual way. What is life? Nothing but an infinite sea and the drops in that sea are people.

Life seems so tremendously beautiful to me now...

...so full - so real and joyous. I am in a world of artists: actors, musicians, writers, painters, sculptors, architects and yes even the landscape gardeners. How did I ever miss becoming a landscape gardener when that was what was hoped for me at first? Because the experience gained in the past lives as an actor (I have found this out about myself) was somewhere stored up in my subconsciousness and had to express itself again in order to overcome some obstacle still left undefeated.

I am so happy in this artist world that I have asked H.P.B. if this is not heaven. She seemed to look through me for a few moments, then her calm eyes deepened into a genial smile. "If you and your artist friends find happiness and contentment here," she said, "then you are in the heaven for the artists.

But remember, little mountain climber" - that is what she called me - "remember that the farmers find also a heaven for farmers; the red Indians, a happy hunting ground and for Buddhists their nirvana."

This statement, as so many of Mme. Blavatsky's seemed to be to be designed to make me think. So I thought it over for a while and came to the conclusion that perhaps I was getting so enthusiastic with my surroundings and friends that I was in danger of becoming contented enough not to look further. I told this to H.P.B., she answered, "You are thinking and learning. Yes, contentment to remain in place causes blindness. Life eternal is a ladder. Climb!"

I have met Luther Burbank. He looked so young and sort of radiant I could scarcely believe it was him when I was told it was he. He came right over to me, because he understood at once how much I admired his work with flowers and fruit. He told me he was not amazed to find a nature world over here and that he fully expected as much.

He said no one could work with the miracles of nature and not come to realize that an after-life of progression existed. Burbank, or later Luther, as he asked me to call him, (everyone seems to be called by their baptismal or nicknames here) is studying plant life the same as ever but with the heightened sight that death brings with the assistance of spirits here who have greater knowledge than he.

Luther Burbank told me how surprised he was to find no insects here. If there are flowers here, I asked him, why are there no insects? He explained that most insects are of a low order in the evolutionary scale of life and they upon death immediately reincarnate into similar forms in order to enlarge by much experience their intelligence. Insects, he said, possessing already a high type of intelligence such as ants and bees are ready upon their death to reincarnate into a higher form of life. So this is the fascinating work out of evolution. I understand much better now.

When I expressed my delight over this to Mr. Burbank he smiled and answered, "Well you and I are now standing on the threshold of knowledge and on the verge of realization; a vista has been opened up to us of the enormity of life and we are for the moment overwhelmed by its sublimity."

I asked him if he would care to visit the earth again very much. He said he most decidedly would and that he was interested in his students there and in their continuance of his work. That as soon as he learned new wonders of life's laws, he intended projecting into the minds of such workers as would be receptive to his influence, the results of his labors. "I will inspire them with my discoveries and so help the world," he said.

So you see this is one of the reasons why disembodied souls return to the earth; to help humanity learn more readily the lessons that will most advance it spiritually.

John Burroughs, too, I have seen. He is also active in studying the nature world. He is often working near and with Mr. Burbank. They link up quite naturally, I have discovered with other naturalists who have gone on before - Audubon and others - just as I am linking up with other artists. Like attracts like and in this way life goes on in circles and every circle, no matter how individual, connects up with others. This is what communicating spirits call the "Chain of Life".

They like to express themselves symbolically H.P.B. says because symbolism is the true language of the soul. I am urged by her and others to tell the facts as I learn them as plainly as I can. They say that earth people become confused and often lose the spirit of the communication when too symbolic or technical language is used. Of course my helpers explain much of these truths to me before I reach you and then I tell in my own way, as best I can.

The force is gone now. I will go on with this another time. Good night.

The Ninth Revelation

Paris, October 1926.

I have seen Harold Lockwood.[62]

It has made me very happy to have met him as he has greatly developed spiritually. I am sure he will be a help to me. He always was serious minded in his earth-life. He is naturally interested in helping the people of his profession to find themselves, so to speak, when they arrive over here.

Harold says that all actors are very child-like in nature and that their naive way of looking at life makes them unusually susceptible to influence good or bad. Their arrival onto the astral plane is a very critical time for them he says. Being usually given over to worldly pleasures and lighthearted fun, they are apt to fall prey to the temptations and allurements of the lower astral plane.

I admit, Natacha, that I have found it very fascinating to visit and watch this particular phase of astral life. In it the material illusions of joy are erroneously magnified and out of proportion.

But so stimulating are these false illusions, empty as shining bubbles, that the participators in them are so tormented by their sharpened appetites that they rush madly back to earth to gratify themselves through mediumistic people. This lower astral plane is glittering but a false paradise, if I may use the expression. A place more brilliant in its highlights than Broadway's whitest glare; a place more somber and ghastly in its shadows than the darkest dives of the Limehouse.

And the ensnaring part of it is that everything seems too actual and real. From this plane, Harold Lockwood says, come all the stories from spirits about tobacco, food, shops and all the rest of it, because these spirits cling too closely to the world to get away from those mundane ideas.

The buildings here are not as I have described those of the higher astral plane. You remember I said those were built of thought force. Well these in the lower astral are of thought-force too but of a much coarser quality.

There is nothing inspired or ethereally beautiful about them. They look almost identical with the buildings of the earth-plane only they are more high-keyed - in some ways more subtle - I think I should say.

There are places there like jazz palaces and night clubs. People who loved such places in the earth-life frequent them. It is sad to see so many souls earth-bound to such ideas.

Here, to the illusive happiness of this plane...

...Harold Lockwood, Wally Reid and Olive Thomas [63] took me with them to visit. You must understand, Natacha, that while we cannot ascend into higher vibrations than we have attained to, we can at will descend into lower, to visit, commune or to help.

There was music - jazz - and a great deal of dancing both good and bad. There was no restraint whatever. People did exactly as they chose. Some sang at the top of their voices. Some shrieked madly. Some flung themselves into the most grotesque postures - sort of solo dances, one might call them. Others told all kinds of stories of drinking and of various vices for the purpose of, I was informed, of exciting their desires.

Whenever people reached what appeared to be the height of their wildest frenzy, they trooped off in great mists of dull red color, brown and reddish orange, eastward to gratify through human beings their frantic desires. Having no longer physical bodies of their own, they are forced to use the bodies of others still living upon earth. H.P.B has told me that earth-people reached and attacked by these earth-bound souls find their own desires and appetites, quite unaccountably to them, literally sweeping them off their feet.

She says their sensations are greatly magnified as they enjoy not only their own but the added sensations of the influencing entities. Now I can understand the real reason for perverts of all kinds - habitual drunkards, drug addicts and degenerates; persons all of them being weak, evil - controlled people.

Harold said that they would come to see the emptiness of it all sooner or later. There are millions of spirits watching and waiting to help their millions of friends who are earth-bound and deluded.

Many people here and probably many of earth who do not quite understand these truths, have wondered at my rapid progress spiritually since my passing over. They do not take into consideration that here time means absolutely nothing and that great progression may come in a single revealing flash of realization.

Many spirits who wonder at my progress have themselves tried to communicate with their earth friends and were barely able to reach them and entirely unable to explain anything of this life to them. These people seem at a loss to account for the fact that I so recently came among them and I can easily go back to the earth and give truths as I learn them.

They do not know that I am able to do this because in my earth-life I was a natural medium and more than a little developed in my mediumship and also that I already knew before death considerable about communication with spirits. I am so glad now that I did know these things. Otherwise, Natacha, I could not so soon have reached you and through you, others.

Harold Lockwood was also very mediumistic in his earth-life and his knowledge of the beyond has helped him immensely, he says, to a more rapid progression. Then, too, we have both been fortunate to have such enlightened helpers. And it is lucky that I have had so clear a medium to express myself through.

Harold says he has often come through mediums in the earth-plane. He says that Virginia Pearson is a medium and he often visits her.

I find that Pola Negri is a mediumistic if she only knew it. She gets very clear first impressions of people and conditions but she seldom follows them. I am sure she felt my presence when she viewed my remains for I went up to her and shook her by the arm and shouted into her ear that I was not dead and that I was very sorry for her grief. But she could not hear me. Yes, Pola is a psychic. That is why she is so temperamental - so impressionistic. I wish she understood.

So many people are psychic more or less.

Nearly everybody. Charlie Chaplin is too. He knows it but would smile if I told him so. He is exceedingly impressionistic and inspirational in his way of working.

Doris Kenyon is another naturally mediumistic person. Not that she actually sees spirits but she is able to hear then with her inner psychic ear. That is why she is able to receive writings from them. I do not mean that she has not talent of her own for writing, she has. But certain spirits are able to inspire her. Ella Wheeler Wilcox says she goes to her.

But there is one person I know who can hardly be called psychic and that is Jimmy Quirk. [64] During the time my body lay on view in New York, I went to his office several times. I always liked Jimmy and I tried to make him realize I was still alive. I touched him. I thumped his desk. I shouted in his ear. But Jimmy did not seem to hear. He was too surrounded by a wall of the hard-and-fast facts of everyday life to be reached psychically. Yet Jimmy's impressions of people are usually right. Somewhere within his complex lingers that psychic spark which under certain conditions might be fanned into a flame.

As we leave the bright illusion world, we pass through some gruesome aspects of life. I was glad that I was with my friends. Black forms jostled us, or rushed by muttering fearfully to themselves; some moaning. Many were weeping and crying aloud. To have seen and heard this misery is the worse thing I have ever experienced.

I wanted to put an end to it. I wanted to tell those souls of the lovely higher astral plane where I am living. It seemed so unjust for these souls to be doomed.

Just as my desire to help them surged like a wave through my whole being, a dark form brushed against me and two arms were thrown around me. A voice called, "Rudy! Rudy!" I stared at the form. Its contact with me seemed to cause it to become faintly illuminated. The shock of recognition which followed caused my whole soul to tremble.

It was the spirit of Bobby Harron! [65] Bobby clung to be as if never to let go again. He seemed frightened and panic-stricken. He gasped like one who had been suffocating. "Give me light! Give me light!" he kept exclaiming just as a person on would would cry out for air.

I did not know what to do. Harold, Wally and Olive Thomas gathered around him. "You are safe now," said Harold. "We have been looking for you. You have asked for light and now we can give it to you."

It was some time before Bobby could calm his excitement. "I went too soon. I went too soon!" he repeated over and over again, speaking of his sudden death.

This touched me so I could not refrain from weeping. But my emotion was that of joy. I was so pleased to have had a share in the rescue. This is the first time that such an occurrence has come my way.

When Bobby grew quiet he told us that ever since his too sudden passing out, he had been in what seemed to him a constant darkness. "But now you will be with us in the light," Harold Lockwood assured him.

Olive Thomas told me she had had almost the same experience. "No one," she said, "who has not gone through it can begin to realize the awfulness of it."

There are many spirits who do nothing else but rescue these earth-bound people. It is their chosen work. I though I would like to do it but I have not been over here long enough for that sort of this yet; Harold tells me.

During the great storms, that swept over Florida and over the sea, I saw many rescuers working with the souls of people who had perish or accidents often do not believe they have left their bodies and the world. They feel that something terrible has happened but they cannot tell just what.

During these great storms I heard strange sounds in the ether or atmosphere, or whatever you call it. If you heard them in the earth-world you would probably think they were great bells tolling. I asked Henry Watts, a guide of the medium's, what those sounds were. He said they were astral signals announcing the coming over of souls from some big earth disaster.

The force is gone. I can't speak any longer. Good night, I will come again soon.

100

The Tenth Revelation

The Atlantic Sea, November, 1926.

I want to talk to you Natacha about my acting.

I have learned more about it since coming here than I ever knew before. I can now look back with a new understanding upon certain incidents that used to perplex me.

This understanding comes from talks which I have had with Charles Frohman and Clyde Fitch. [66] These men know the psychic truths about acting and writing. Both men are still vitally interested in the theater and in writing for it. They are also interested in inspiring earth-people to write for it. Their knowledge of the subject has helped me greatly.

Mr. Fitch says that the characters in a novel or play become as the writer's mind evolved them, real, living entities! The writer, according to the degree of his powers of visualization, holds the form of his characters so concentratedly in mind, that a real mental body for them is formed. Into this mental body the force of his creative facilities pours the emotional qualities necessary to endow it with an individuality. In this way a distinct personality is built up.

The building up of this body form, held so strongly in the writer's mind, begins to attract to itself astral substance and it also absorbs from the writer himself ectoplasm and auric emanations. This is all rather hard for me to say, but H.P.B. is helping me and I hope I am giving it to you in an understandable way.

In this way an astral envelope is gradually formed. The writer's thought-entity enters it and finally the creation detaches itself from the brain and goes on living an independent, though limited existence.

So you can see, Natacha, that these character creations of an author are in truth his brainchildren who have been conceived, gestated and born. This is a true creation, H.P.B. says, and she told me that this is the way the power called God creates offspring; through thought.

Clyde Fitch went on to explain to me how very often writers dreaded getting at the job of producing characterizations. And now I see this to be the reason for it; they dread the labor and birth of their astrally materialized creations.

H.P.B. explained that these mind creations are limited in the scope of their activities to the degree of development to which the writer had brought them. They possess souls inasmuch as they have within them a spark thrown off from the soul-fire of their author, who himself is but a much more highly developed spark thrown off from the fire of God. These thought entities are entirely without previous experience being able to express only the part laid out for them in the story by the writer and what independent thought action they may possess is also constricted to that circle.

When such a thought character becomes known to the reading world, talked about, thought over, hated or loved, it may continue to exist as an independent entity for years; for as long as human interest may feed it and thus keep it alive. But when thought characters are unimportant and unaccepted or soon forgotten by the world, their existence is a short one. They fade out, as it were, and are dematerialized and reabsorbed into the great plane of ideas.

H.P.B. says the stronger among these thought entities sometimes manifest in a séance, when people who might attract them are present and they are even able to speak through the medium. They can readily be detected, however, as they usually appear with an artificial ring to their vague utterances. Often they express themselves in a line or two of dramatic intensity borrowed from the story world to which they belong.

Clairvoyant eyes can sometimes see them.

On account of this they may sometimes be confused with real spirits. They usually look to be smaller or else much larger than genuine spirits. They become enlarged in form and power by the public thought force of many years being focused upon them.

Now I will show you how this curious race of thought beings (for their is a whole race of them) connects with my acting. I say "my" acting because I take myself as an example, knowing my own experience better than others.

Whenever I used to read over a script that interested me, I began to concentrate my whole attention upon the character I was to portray. The first reading or two never seemed to do more than awaken within me a responsive interest in the role. The reading of the part was only like getting a more or less hazy outline of the possibilities the characterization afforded.

But it was when I was away from the script when I was by myself, sometimes during the day, more often at night, the stranger side of acting presented itself to me. Once I had read the part I was to play I could think of nothing else. What I then took to be a mental vision of how the character should look (but what I now know to have been a clairvoyant view, through my mediumistic powers of the thought-entity created by the writer of the story) haunted me day and night. I could not free myself from it nor did I want to for the sake of the work, even though I was then ignorant of the true conditions of the matter.

Clyde Fitch says that actors who are only slightly mediumistic easily throw off the influence of the thought-entity when they are not actually working the part. But you see, I was a real medium by nature and instead of being able to shake off the control of the entity, I fell more and more under its compelling spell as my interest grew.

Clinging tenaciously to my super-sensitive responsiveness the thought-entity quickly merged itself into my very being where for the time it became the life of my life and dominated entirely my actions. It was my gift of impressionable negativeness being controlled by the living, character-entity as it worked out its life-mission in its little world of the story.

For the duration of the entity's control my individuality slumbered. I know that often it surprised you to find me carrying out the details of a characterization when away from the studio in the quietness of our home life. But that curious facility - gift - of mediumship was what made me as good an actor as I was.

Another psychic phase of acting is this. Sometimes certain spirits got to a writer and project the picture of themselves into his brain so that he works them almost subconsciously into his story. Mr. Fitch says this only happens when the play or novel is important to cause the spirits to feel it is really worth while to reach earth-humanity in this way. These writings are those with some great message to the world.

Charles Frohman says that all writers are mediums, that is all writers who give any kind of message to their work. Their concentration makes them a center of magnetic force which facilitates spirits to project any help they may have to offer the writer to the world.

Actors are often inspired while playing by the very spirit who impressed the part upon the writer. When the actor is really mediumistic, as all great actors are whether they know it or not, the spirit may actually play the part through him.

Sarah Bernhardt has told me that this was often the case with her and that she knew it. Duse, too, says she was very sensitive to such influences and that that was the reason for her ability to play tremendous roles when she wandered about Italy as a child.

Life, Natacha, holds many truths that seem like wonders until we come to understand them. Then they appear to be what they really are and perfectly natural occurrences.

Charlie Frohman says that this element of mediumship in me would have developed as time went on into a much keener sense of receptivity until I should have become such a responsive instrument to these impelling entities that I should have been able to portray with ease really great roles. But that happiness, for some good reason, never fear, has been denied to me in this last earth-incarnation. Another time perhaps.

Here, with enlightened knowledge and with understanding of the true facts and with such intelligent helpers and advisers around me, I know I shall be able to forge ahead with the beautiful art which means more to me than life itself; somehow. Oh, I am so glad that does not rob us of the power to go on and on. How dreadful it would be to have to lie cold and lifeless in a grave until some far-off judgment day summoned us to life again. By that time I am sure I should have forgotten all I ever knew about acting!

Now, in the midst of this glory of onliving, in this heaven of work continuance, I see how those teachings of my childhood were utterly preposterous.

Oh, Natacha, think of it - life -sweet, loving, helpful and friendly, progressive and continuing on for ever - is it not magnificent? Is it not God? To me it is like the greatest burst of melody one could imagine.

Cara mia, the force is waning. I must let go of the medium and slip away. I will come again soon. Buona Notte.

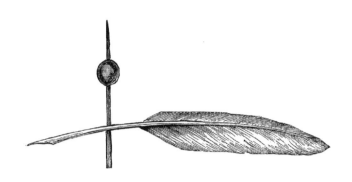

The Eleventh Revelation

The Atlantic Sea, November 1926.

It may surprise you to know...
...that I have met Curley [67] over here. You remember, he was the animal trainer. I was very glad to see him and he certainly seemed pleased at meeting me.

A curious thing about Curley is that I cannot look at him without seeing his aura. There is a lot of red in it and orange. I do not see everyone's aura but Curley's is so vibrant that it becomes outstanding. When I spoke to him about it he did not seem to understand. He said, that if there were colors around him he did not know it and so far as he knew no one else had ever seen them before.

Of course we talked about animals. Curley knows more about them now than he ever did in his earth-life as his vision is not so limited in this plane. He is not in the higher astral plane but he is not earth-bound.

Curley feels if he had only known more about psychic influence before he died he would have had much better results with animals. He has been shown by his "helpers" that it was detrimental to his own development to have to resort at time to harsh methods.

But this did not really hold Curley back because in his heart he was not unkind. He always tried kindness until he saw that an animal was too vicious to respond. I asked him if he thought it was a wise thing to try and train wild animals. According to his "helpers" it is not unless kind methods only can be employed.

Curley is not studying animals from a psychic viewpoint which shows them up in an altogether different light. He finds them far more open to astral influences than is man. Truly psychic people often tap planes beyond the astral and so pass it by.

But animals and also primitive people are close to the currents of the earth and of the lower astral plane. Curley has learned that the earth is filled with magnetism and the atmosphere with electricity. He notices that animals respond to these forces more readily than human beings.

He divides the animal world (leaving man out of it as a distinctly different type of being although using an animal-like body) into these divisions; reptiles (including fish and insects), mammals and fowl.

The reptiles, according to Curley, draw their motive power from the magnetism to the earth when it is warmed by the friction of the rays of the sun. That is why they are either legless or else have but very short legs. Nature requires them to lie flat upon the earth a large part of the time in order to absorb and sustain currents. Food is taken much less frequently by reptiles than by mammals because it only provides sustenance for their bodily growth; they do not depend on it for motive power. Snakes, especially, are often more active after a long fast.

In winter, when the magnetic forces are less active and the electric currents more powerful, reptiles become unable to absorb enough earth magnetism to remain active and so lie dormant until the forces are renewed. Psychically, winter seems to be a sort of recharging time.

Not only reptiles but also some of the animals - for instance bears and woodchucks go into this trance-like winter sleep. Curley finds such animals who do so to be almost non-meat eating. Creatures that hibernate crawl into caves or holes deep in the earth as possible where what magnetism they are able to contact keeps them charged with the vital currents of life.

This is all most interesting to me.

Curley does not tell it to me in technical terms and I would not understand if he did. So I am telling it to you in the same simple way trusting I am making it understandable to all.

Curley says insects and lizards draw their magnetism from plants and trees which are always highly charged. He says that is why wet trees are so often struck by lightening. He thinks from what he has learned on the astral plane that many insects are much more highly evolved than reptiles and many mammals.

I asked John Burroughs about this too. He is a dear friend of the medium's mother and it was she who first brought me into contact with him. Mr. Burroughs laughed and said that the trouble with science was that under it everything was too strictly classified; too mechanically, too materialistically labeled. It all comes down to a matter of viewpoint, he explained. A scientist either looks at things through materialistic eyes or through psychic eyes.

If he uses the former method he accounts for only what actually appears to lie before him. He forgets, too, that before the invention of the microscope he neither saw nor believed many of the things he does now. Men do not like to believe what they do not see until some instrument is invented to make what was invisible, visible.

He forgets also, with all his eyes and microscopes to see, the main thing still remains unseen - the very force binding the atoms of the specimen together, the vitality which animates it - the life-current. The most important thing of all; the power which has produced whatever visible, tangible, material proofs his physical eyes may see, that power itself remains unrevealed to material eyes. Greater than must be the unseen than the seen.

With material eyes we view the effect but the cause is only perceived psychically. So the materialist is balked at the very beginning but he is usually too pig-headed to admit it.

When the scientist has learned the psychic truth of these matters he realizes that true classification depends upon the degree of development to which the specimens have attained. For instance, some insects are more intelligent than many men. Ants, bees, wasps - are they not more intelligent in their work group, in their industry than many men from the lower walks of humanity en masse?

Among animals, how many there are, especially dogs whose loyalty, faithfulness and courage have gone far beyond those qualities in certain human beings. What number of horses there have been whose fine intelligence has saved many a human life when conditions prevented that human intelligence from seeing its way.

And to think there are people so callow, so stupid as to say these creatures have no souls. They have souls. Death has taught me, Natacha, that everything created by God - all things animate or seemingly inanimate - are possessed of souls. But they are all in different stages of evolution.

It is, of course, a great deal of joy to me to learn that animals live on. John Burroughs explained that intelligent animals and birds often remain in the astral plane for considerable time before reincarnating. Some teachers claim, he said, that animal life at the change called death merges back into what is called the animal group-soul. But Mr. Burroughs says that is only true of unevolved animal life.

Animals, absorbing through close association with men more or less of his intelligence, step out from the mass of animal life and become individualized. These, at death, are not absorbed into the animal group-soul but go on independently, progressing through many incarnations up the gradual scale of life.

Such animals with their

beginning of soul development often have keen sight of things in the astral. Dogs, cats, parrots, horses and elephants often clairvoyantly see spirits. And spirits are often able to influence animals accomplishing seeming miracles. What power is it that guides a horse to ride through the blinding terror of a blizzard? It is the guiding hand of the rider's guardian spirit leading the psychic horse onward to safety.

Why do dogs so often howl before the death of some member of the family? Is it just coincidence? No. It is because the dog's psychic faculties sense the subtle change that is commencing in the physical organism of the person who nears the hour of change. That change being the loosening of spirit from body which gives off a peculiar vibration which startles and alarms the dog.

Henry Watts says this death vibration may be seen as a color; a mauve grey. It may also be heard as a sound and a continuous low sighing whistle. And it may be smelled as an uncannily permeating odor.

There are so many things to learn about this life. I am only touching on the verge of them. This is all I have learned about animals so far but as time goes on and I learn more I hope to be able to come back and share my knowledge with you, Natacha, and with others.

Now let me tell you about "Sheik".

One of the first things I saw after I passed over was this dear old police dog. You know how much he loved me and how he always pined for me whenever I left him.

You know how I did leave him and how, on account of home-sickness for me - the poor fellow died. I am truly sorry for that. I know it was very wrong of me leaving poor "Sheik" to pine away when with little extra trouble I might have taken him with me. I have certainly found out here, where so many belated lessons are learned, how wrong I was. I have also found out that there are unwritten laws governing every one of our actions, good or bad.

I was feeling pretty lonely and not yet used to my new surroundings when as if to bid me welcome, I saw the quizzical eyes, the pointed ears and the wagging tail of "Sheik". I was overjoyed. He seemed a friend in need. But just as I rushed up to put my arms around him, he disappeared and I was left alone. I felt as if I had been struck. Then it dawned upon me that perhaps this is the way poor "Sheik" felt when I had left him behind.

I felt a touch on my arm. Turning around I saw H.P.B. standing beside me. Her eyes seemed to burn right through me.

"What does it mean?" I asked her.

H.P.B. replied something like this - "One of life's lessons, my boy. You neglected that dog and he died for love of you. Because of this you

108

will not be able to have him with you again until you have earned the right. It is the law of karma."

I felt awfully ashamed. But I hope soon to be able to have him again. One consolation is that I know Curley is keeping "Sheik" for me.

I thought you might be glad to know this about "Sheik". Remember, Natacha, if we attach animals to ourselves we owe a responsibility to them. We are their guardian spirits.

The force is weakening. I must go. Good night, Natacha, good night.

America Reacts to Rudolph Valentino's *Revelations*

Natacha's unwavering confidence in the authenticity of Rudy's "Revelations" was met with widespread, mixed emotions. The news she was co-authoring a book with her deceased ex-husband made front page headlines for a day or two in almost every newspaper from *The New York Times* to *The Morning Register* in Eugene, Oregon.

To cynical non-believers shaking their heads over their morning coffee and newspapers, Natacha Rambova had just lost her mind. There was little gray area in the acceptance of Natacha's other-worldy manuscript. Either it was scoffed at as ridiculous fantasy or embraced as definitive proof of life-after-death.

As Natacha clarified Rudy had nothing significant to say from the astral plane in regards to Pola Negri, "La Negri" issued her swift response. This prompted more headlines as America stayed tuned for an imminent confrontation between Rudy's last two lovers.

"...'Profane and commercial!' breathed Pola from her Hollywood castle as she read the messages. 'Shocking and profane,' were even added as she registered indignation and mayhaps envy. In fact Pola would intimate that Natacha has been breaking astral confidences. And what is more and worse, Pola was not even mentioned in these astral tête-a-têtes." [68]

Natacha did not stoop to pick up Pola's gauntlet, so the Hollywood press pursued Rudy's first wife Jean Acker for her reaction.

"Rudy did not believe in spirit messages," said Ms. Acker, "He was intelligent and if such messages were received by his second wife, they were too sacred to broadcast." [69]

Among Natacha's more outraged critics was Bess Houdini, the widow of prestidigitator Harry Houdini. Houdini died shortly after Rudy, also succumbing to post-surgical sepsis. Houdini died after advertising he could absorb any blow to the abdomen. This proved not to be the case. Bess Houdini reported she also received messages via mediums allegedly from her late husband. Unlike Natacha, the widow Houdini left no doubt how she felt about those messages.

"I considered them an insult to my intelligence. Miss Rambova's accounts of the antics of the dead seem sacrilegious to me." [70]

Appreciation of "Revelations" would be expressed by Natacha's New York Theosophical acquaintances and her fellow Saturday Nighters. Many of them participated in George's séances and held faith in his abilities as a medium. They also acknowledged as legitimate the subject of communing with the dead from the astral plane.
With the furor leaning predominately in favor of those ridiculing Natacha for inspiring the "row over spirit talk",[71] *When Love Grows Cold's* director Harry O. Hoyt issued a statement in her support. Hoyt's statement appeared in the news a few days after Pola Negri, Jean Acker and Mrs. Harry Houdini's criticisms and did not garner first page coverage. It read in part,

"I had never taken any particular interest in séances, although I have attended the average number and come away cold. However both Clive Brook and myself came away from that séance feeling the man (George Wehner) told us things no one knew but ourselves. Miss Hudnut, I think is and always has been very much in love with Valentino. And knowing her sincerity and Wehner's ability, I feel sure that she could get some kind of messages from the other plane."[72]

Despite being the target of skeptics, Rudy's "Revelations" inspired spiritual discourse and many a sermon was delivered on the possibility of life after death. As wire services dutifully issued the reports, some columnists were unable to resist the mocking; such as the author of one column titled, "Over Teacups".

"Will wonders ever cease? After all the pomp and show prior to the disposition of the earthly remains of the late Valentino, we find that he simply won't stay put. He is back again as a citizen of the astral plane." [73]

"Revelations" proved a daring theosophical move for Natacha. The attribution of one half of her book to psychic messages from movie star, Rudolph Valentino, made the theosophical aspects of it all very Hollywood indeed. Was Natacha assigning the role of mahatma to Rudolph Valentino?

The curious cross-over interests of Rudy's grieving fans and theosophic spiritualists created a quizzical demographic of readers; all enthralled by Natacha Rambova's production of, "Blavatsky and Valentino Together on the Astral Plane!"

The authenticity of "Revelations" is still questioned and surely always will be depending on one's beliefs. Were Natacha Rambova and George Wehner insane, were they of sound mind or were they prophets? For those closest to Natacha, "Revelations" remained a long love letter which she received from Rudy as he crossed over. No one who loved her blamed her for allowing George to keep Rudy alive long enough for her to survive the reality of her loss.

The New York Evening Graphic's Composographs [74]

All the criticism and mockery in the world did not dampen Natacha's resolve. She sought a publisher for her book which she originally titled, *Rudolph Valentino Intime*.[75] She would later change the title to, *Rudy, An Intimate Portrait of Rudolph Valentino by His Wife Natacha Rambova*. As promised, the second half of her book was attributed to Rudolph Valentino; those "Revelations" transmitted from the astral plane.

News that Natacha Rambova was shopping a new manuscript garnered the immediate interest of Bernarr MacFadden. The eclectic health and fitness guru was the publisher of many popular magazines such as *True Story, Physical Culture* and the newspaper tabloid, *The New York Evening Graphic* and consequently held a broad reading audience captive. On MacFadden's invitation,[76] George met with the publisher on Natacha's behalf. MacFadden presented the medium with a proposition; he would publish Rudy's

115

"Revelations" in his tabloid in serial format as a means to advertise the full volume.

Despite Bernarr MacFadden wielding unquestioning power in the publishing world, his *Evening Graphic* was reputed to be the lowest of the low in tabloid journalism. The *Graphic's* sensational content was irresistible with its coverage being primarily sex, crime and scandal; everything from a good hanging to a raid on a speakeasy with lavish illustration.

These illustrations were often created in the form of shocking composographs. A composograph was a graphically generated image, a sort of collage or precursor of Adobe Photoshop. Bernarr MacFadden alleged these brazen cut and paste news photos were not necessarily created to fool the public, but to illustrate a story.

"The *Graphic* did things with photographs that respectable newspapers wouldn't think of doing...the *Graphic* was most famous (or infamous) for its composographs; often startling front page images created in the art department by cutting and pasting the faces of celebrities onto the bodies of often scantily-clad models posed to illustrate some real life scene where a camera simply couldn't go..." [77]

Despite the *Graphic's* awful reputation, MacFadden was successful in convincing George and Natacha to test the waters by allowing him to first publish "Revelations".

Natacha should have seen it coming; MacFadden's penchant for a ripe composograph opportunity. At the time of Rudolph Valentino's death the previous August, the *Graphic's* picture editor, Frank Mallen created several notable composographs to exploit the star's passing.[78] One image depicted actors dressed as medical personnel posing in a hospital operating room with "Rudy" prone under a sheet on the operating table. Frank Mallen created additional composographs depicting Rudy in his coffin, of Pola Negri paying her tearful tribute and even the funeral procession.

By creating fake images, the issues of the *Graphic* with the cover composograph of Valentino's funeral procession were selling on the streets of New York City just as the actual procession began. Confused participants in that procession were buying copies of the *Graphic* to see if they could find themselves in the photograph. [79]

When MacFadden's first installment of Rudolph Valentino's "Revelations" hit the streets it was obvious he had taken full advantage. Natacha and George were speechless. On St. Patrick's Day, March 17, 1927, the *Graphic* devoted a full cover page composograph in the day's final Five Star issue to Rudy, wearing a white robe, standing next to Enrico Caruso overlooking a vista of heaven's souls portrayed as a panoramic perspective of scampering humanity.

Natacha and George were mortified and protested the exploitation to Bernarr MacFadden. George lamented saying the images, "..nearly broke our hearts but which we were powerless to stop." [80] MacFadden forged on to publish another installment which displayed a composograph of Rudy, again in heavenly robe conversing face-to-face with Helena Blavatsky.

When MacFadden sent news to Natacha and George reporting how sales of the "Revelations" editions were titanic, their anguish over the tacky composographs was tempered. The response, good or bad was overwhelming and people were eagerly reading Rudy's words from the astral plane whether they believed them to be authentic or not.

The *Graphic's* exposure of "Revelations" was a profitable ploy for MacFadden but Natacha did not grant him the honor of publishing her book. She would decide on Hutchinson and Company of Paternoster Row in London. Although resoundingly sneered at by cynics, her book was generally well-received. With her account of life as Rudolph Valentino's wife providing a juicy glimpse into the rarefied world of the Valentino marriage, even "Revelations" critics tolerated their inclusion in the book. In London, Sir Arthur Conan Doyle reported he was hard-pressed to keep the book stocked in his bookstore.

Recognizing the public's interest, *Photoplay* magazine featured an article by Frederick James Smith titled, *"Does Valentino Speak?"* in their February 1926 issue. The magazine posted a disclaimer stating that their publication of the article was not the magazine's endorsement of life after death. In the article Natacha reiterated how Rudy watched his own funeral and how he was frustrated attempting to speak to his friends as they processed by his coffin in Campbell's Funeral Home. She advised his public by saying that when their adulation waned, he would be free to become more absorbed in astral world activities saying,

" He (Rudy) wants earth-people to know and realize that there is no death and no separation. He wants earth-people to miss his heartrending experience. He wants them to realize and believe in the beauty and perfection of this after-life." [81]

The *Photoplay* article, replete with an image of Natacha's face gazing into a crystal ball was presented as her unwavering defense of "Revelations" and an overt expression of her love for Rudy.

New Love

In the spring of 1927, Natacha made an appearance in a courtroom as a reporter covering the Snyder-Gray murder trial. The reportage of her courtroom sighting primarily detailed her wardrobe; with one mention on April 22 reporting she wore a "black tailored dress, black, tight fitting hat and a black and white fox fur." [82] She was then also set to debut in her next stage performance; a play initially titled, *"The Triple Cross"*. After a short run in Boston and Connecticut, the title was changed to *"Set a Thief"* and the production opened in New York to lackluster reviews. Natacha received kudos for being gorgeous, but her acting was panned as being "mannequin". [83]

At this time, Natacha leased an apartment over a storefront at 58 West 55th Street and there opened a couture dress boutique. She would sell her own designs and cater to an exclusive clientele, including many of her Hollywood acquaintances.

"Natacha Rambova; the name in letters of stone appear above a shop next to Fifth Avenue...Rich fabrics and pieces of antique jewelry are in the window, beyond which your curious gaze is lost in folds of gauzy green..." [84]

There, Natacha designed day dresses, evening gowns, accessories, jewelry and fabric and pursued the development of her own make up line. [85]

It was then she wrote her one play titled, *All That Glitters*. In this literary endeavor no medium was needed, no spirit guides channeled and no dearly-departed consulted. Natacha devised her screenplay herself in an effort to torch the last remnant of her Hollywood life by creating her characters as obvious movie stars she'd known.

Characters not so subtly cast as Mary Pickford, Gloria Swanson, George Ullman and Rudy himself were written into her plot line and as near libel. Natacha's character, as Alice, is firmly established as heroine and she heroically rescues her immature husband. The play would not serve as a true revenge because *All That Glitters* was never produced or published and had no audience. It did serve instead as her definitive and then private word on her Hollywood experience and marriage to Rudolph Valentino. In "Revelations" she mourned Rudy's death and the loss of their love, in *All That Glitters* she vindicated herself of the entire affair. When her mother finished reading her daughter's play, she wept and demanded Natacha burn every copy.[86] Natacha did no such thing.

With the catharsis of its completion, Natacha moved on. She was seen out and about at many Manhattan social events and always wearing her finest haute couture designs. At the Thomas Wilfred Clavilux recital at the Graybar building, a teenage boy, Mark Hasselriis remembers being star-struck by the visage of the beautiful woman wearing a turban who arrived as he recalled, "with a middle age woman." [87] This middle-aged woman accompanying Natacha that evening was Alice Bailey.

Natacha met Alice Bailey through her affiliations with the New York Theosophical Society and in theosophy the two women found friendship. Alice Bailey was the founder of the Arcane School, a theosophical educational institution providing world-wide "training in the science of the soul."[88] Alice Bailey authored twenty-four enormous tomes on various theosophical subjects with titles such as *Esoteric Healing, The Seven Rays of Life* and *A Treatise on White Magic*. Alice would best be remembered for first coining the phrase "New Age".

Alice Bailey alleged her lengthy books were telepathically dictated to her by a mahatma, just as Helena Blavatsky alleged her *Secret Doctrine* was dictated to her by her mahatma and as Natacha claimed in the creation of "Revelations".

Natacha's friendship with Alice Bailey represented a significant change in course regarding her esoteric interests. It was Alice who first introduced Natacha to New York's trendiest school of esoteric thought; the Roerich Society. The Roerich Society was founded in New York City in 1921 by two Russians, husband and wife, Nicholas and Helena Roerich. Their society was established as the Master Institute of United Arts and similar to Alice Bailey's Arcane School, the curriculum offered classes in all aspects of esoterica, art and religion.

Nicholas Roerich commanded his society from an imposing position as world-renown scholar, author and accomplished artist of spiritual landscape oil paintings depicting his treks through India and the Altai region of the Himalayas. His dedication to world order through art and peaceful political solutions would earn him a nomination for the Nobel Peace Prize in 1929, presented by the University of Paris.

His wife, Helena was also renown as an author and authority on theosophical thought. She, as Blavatsky, Natacha Rambova and Alice Bailey alleged her writings were transcribed to her by mahatmas. Helena held as much authority in the Roerich Society initiatives as her husband, wrote prolifically and was and still is revered within the Roerich international community. During the 1920's, the theosophical New York community embraced Helena and Nicholas' Society as a chic new direction both philosophically and socially.

Helena and Nicholas Roerich had two sons, George and Svetoslav. It would be Svetoslav who would rise to leadership within the society being strikingly handsome with a dashing demeanor and personal style which served him well. He studied art and architecture at New York's Columbia University and as an artist he rivaled his father's technical ability with the oils. A fashionable young gentleman sporting a goatee and tailored, tweed jackets, he exuded a palpable self-assurance; an appeal all the more mesmerizing being steeped in the metaphysical.

The attraction between Natacha and "Svetie" as she called him, evolved quickly into an affair with the role of Natacha's rebound love falling to the Roerich heir apparent. Natacha and Svetie merged over their passion for all things theosophical and were soon engaged to be married.

While Natacha and Svetoslav planned their life together, George Wehner met the love of his life, Alex Rotov. Alex (a.k.a. Alexis) Rotov was a ballet dancer and a popular personality in New York's bohemian art scene.[89] Russian by birth, his family moved to New York in 1907 when he was five years old. He studied ballet for fourteen years with Ivan Clustine, Mikhail Mordkin and Olga Preobrajenska and alleges to have received a scholarship granted by Anna Pavlova.

Alex Rotov was, by the late 1920's, an accomplished and well-known dancer. However, Alex's five-foot-one height[90] prevented him from being cast in lead classical dance roles. He instead starred in comedic parts in which he enjoyed his success; consistently finding work and gaining notoriety for his niche performances.

In May of 1927, George and his new love Alex embarked on a trip to Europe[91] where they toured the Azores, Madeira, Sicily, Greece and Egypt. They would be gone for nearly one year. George and Alex visited Muzzie and Uncle Dickie at the chateau at Juan les Pins in the summer of 1927 and traveled on to Switzerland to visit Paul Ivanovitch in his home in Vienna.

Meanwhile, in New York, Natacha was preparing for her next stage appearance. Despite her deep disappointment with the F.B.O. film *When Love Grows Cold* and two uneventful appearances in *The Purple Vial* and *Set a Thief,* she still entertained thoughts of a career in acting. In September of 1927, she appeared in a play which was set in the Louisiana Bayou titled, *Creoles.*

"*Creoles* was...a romantic comedy drama...which opened at the Klaw Theater. Despite a spectacular New Orleans set designed by Norman Bel Geddes, the plot of *Creoles*-which focused on a convent-bred girl, Jacinta, and her infatuation with a Caribbean pirate-left the critics cold."[92]

Natacha Goes Wholesale

Throughout 1927 and 1928, Natacha continued to be Leslie Grant Scott's devoted student of theosophy. Her engagement to Svetoslav inspired her to broaden her studies to embrace all Roerich philosophies which advanced theosophy by including doctrines of world peace and the international veneration and protection of art and nature. While delving deeper into this academia, Natacha lived as Svetie's muse. He would sketch and paint her portrait many times, enjoying a uniquely personal artistic vantage point as her lover.

In 1928, Nicholas and Helena Roerich moved to the Kullu Valley in India, leaving Svetoslav in charge of the Roerich Society's New York interests. His responsibilities included the management of the Master Institute of Arts as well as overseeing final preparations for the opening of the Master Building; the Roerich Society's prestigious skyscraper at 310 Riverside Drive. The Master Building was set to become a center for arts and philosophical study and it would not only provide apartments and studios for working artists but house a museum on the first three floors.[93] This museum would be co-founded and managed by Natacha and Svetoslav.

Their ambitious *Museum of Religion and Philosophy* was scheduled to open in January of 1930. In their museum prospectus materials, the "Officers" and "Advisory Board" read as a "Who's Who" of the theosophical movement in Manhattan at the time. Svetoslav Roerich would be President and Leslie Grant Scott, Vice-President. Leslie would share the position with her husband R.T.M. Scott, who was nominated as chairman of the museum's "Scientific Psychic Research" section. This section of the museum would include classes on telepathy, clairvoyance, thought forms, auras and more. Natacha would act as the museum's Secretary-Treasurer.

The museum's advisory committee included Alice Bailey as well as Nicholas Roerich and this surely did not please Helena Roerich. Helena was a fierce opponent of Alice Bailey and a certain jealousy seems to have existed between the two matriarchs of New York's theosophical world. Helena accused Alice of appropriating Roerich curriculum for use in her Arcane School and debunked Alice's other-wordly mahatma as being an impostor.

Natacha and Svetie walked a thin line in befriending Alice Bailey and appointing her to a position on their Roerich Society museum's advisory committee. The rivalry between Alice Bailey and Helena Roerich was an aggressive one, steeped in accusations of an arcane nature. Helena Roerich believed Alice Bailey was appropriating her mahatma and misrepresenting him as her own master. It appears Helena took the subject of mahatma appropriation more seriously than did Alice Bailey, her son Svetoslav or the woman he was about to marry, Natacha Rambova.

Meanwhile on the Riviera, George and Alex faced complications while visiting the chateau in Juan les Pins. George collapsed from what would be referred to as psychic exhaustion with his condition so grave he required hospitalization. He attributed his illness to the strenuous psychological effort required to maintain a deep-trance for his clientele.

Muzzie and Uncle Dickie Hudnut assumed responsibility for George's recovery and escorted him by train to Paris for medical evaluation and care. They established residency at the Hotel Saint Rafael during his hospitalization in Paris. When Muzzie and Uncle Dickie returned to the Riviera, George remained in Paris with Alex until he was deemed well enough to travel. He and Alex returned to New York on May 1st, 1928 with the Hudnuts arriving on a different ship the same day. [94]

122

Muzzie remained protective of George's fragile condition and upon their arrival, she escorted him on a few weeks vacation to San Francisco, Los Angeles and Salt Lake City.

It was during this summer of 1928, when Natacha announced her dress shop was so successful she was expanding into the wholesale business. This news garnered headlines as she granted lengthy interviews in which she expounded on her theory of color in regards to women's wear.

"Miss Rambova, in her New York studio, creates personality costumes and maintains that color preferences reveal the character of wearers. Her own mode of dress gives her an Oriental aura and whats more seems exactly to suit her type. 'Dressing to suit one's type,' you will soon learn is a phrase and an idea taboo with Miss Rambova. She believes in dressing to suit personality and thinks the word 'type' overworked to the point of exhaustion.

Natacha Rambova, who confesses that she likes Persian and Hindu effects, when interviewed on colors and their significance, wore a soft gray frock cut on straight, original lines and with an embroidered bodice in an odd shade of blue. But blue and gray she explained were not her colors and were simply being worn for experimental purposes.

'Life is color. We vibrate it all the time though we are not conscious of it,' began Miss Rambova as she sat surrounded by colorful Chinese screens, rich tapestries, Oriental vases and handsome gowns and coats of rich fabrics and of her own designing." [95]

Mr. Mundy and His Soon-To-Be Fifth Wife Arrive

It was also during the summer of 1928, when Natacha's friend from Los Angeles, the prolific adventure novelist and ardent theosophist, Talbot Mundy arrived in New York City. Natacha and Muzzie knew Talbot Mundy from their affiliation with the west coast theosophical organization at Point Loma, California of which Mundy was an influential member. Many of Mundy's novels, such as *Om: The Secret of Ahbor Valley* and *The Devils Guard*, included theosophical and occult themes.

When Mundy arrived in Manhattan with his soon-to-be fifth wife, Dawn Allen, they soon joined the Roerich Society. Natacha and

Svetoslav recruited them into the planning of the *Museum of Religion and Philosophy* with Talbot Mundy listed in the museum's brochure as a member of the "Advisory Committee". Talbot Mundy and Dawn Allen also hosted frequent séances for their fellow theosophists in their Greenwich Village apartment.

"For months, from fall to winter, Talbot, Dawn, Natacha and a court stenographer gathered one night a week with George Wehner." [96]

While George's recovery progressed, he penned a memoir titled, *A Curious Life* with Talbot Mundy writing the introduction for the quizzical volume and assisting him in finding a publisher.

In October, shocking news arrived from Juan les Pins; Richard Hudnut died unexpectedly from heart failure. The beloved and fabulously wealthy Uncle Dickie would bequeath all but four thousand dollars of his fortune to Muzzie and his adopted step-daughter Natacha. [97]

In January of 1929, Svetoslav traveled to India where he would remain until May visiting his family on their estate in Kullu Valley. Talbot Mundy and Dawn Allen also departed that spring on a European vacation with George. They invited him to accompany them as they were curious to witness his psychic interpretations. [98]

"Wehner accompanied the couple; Talbot was curious to observe his reactions, since he had reported observing numerous psychic phenomena during his trip to Europe with Natacha three years earlier. They toured London, then went on to Rome via Paris, seeing the churches and the ruins." [99]

The end of May, Natacha would sail again for France. She traveled to Paris to design the sets and costumes for a one act opera performed by the American Opera at the Theater Champs Elyseés. The opera libretto was written by the actress Minnie Maddern Fiske and the musical score by W. Franke Harling with the sets also attributed to designer Patrick Morgan. [100]

The opera opened on June 20, 1929 with opinions divided on its jazzy theme. There would be four performances before the opera closed after accumulating $40,000 in debt. [101]

Natacha returned to New York just in time for a meeting of the Friends of the Roerich Museum [102]on August 18, 1929, where she was elected as an officer.

The Master Building & George Attempts Suicide

On October 17, 1929, the Roerich Society's Master Building finally opened at 310 Riverside Drive in Manhattan. Natacha, Svetie, George and Alex, Talbot Mundy and Dawn Allen all leased apartments in the building.[103] Many members of the New York theosophical society also began tenancies in the upscale building as it was advertised as a prestigious center for the arts and esoteric sciences. The intent of the venture was to inspire its tenants to higher creativity and purpose. In this, the Master Building was an immediate success. Even George would feel sufficiently recovered to resume conducting his séances which were often held in Svetie's Master Building penthouse apartment.[104]

As Dawn Allen was a classically-trained musician, she was impressed by the quality of George's pre-trance whistling and the melodies he often hummed during his séances. She and Donna Shinn Russell embarked on a project to transcribe George's music and compose lyrics. Natacha organized a recital for the two women with Dawn playing the piano and Donna singing.

Although George knew about this recital in advance and was given credit as composer, in the days following the event he grew increasingly furious. He accused Dawn Allen and Donna Russell of appropriating his compositions and insisting on some sort of compensation or a public retraction. His aggressive demands generated ill-will; especially in regards to his friendship with Talbot Mundy.

In the wake of George's nervous breakdown the previous year, his deep-trance process changed radically. Dawn Allen would recall how during this time George seemed to be under the control of something unsettling. His temper flew, he was at times vicious and his séance process intensified. Instead of rolling his head side to side he would bang his head uncontrollably on the chair, with his abdomen swelling and manifesting violent reactions. [105]

During what would be his last séance with Talbot Mundy, Dawn Allen and Natacha, held on the skyscraper terrace of Svetoslav Roerich's penthouse apartment in the Master Building, George called out that he was possessed by the spirit of a suicidal man and ran to the edge of the terrace to leap to his death.

Dawn was seated near the terrace railing and grabbed George. She caught him in time but came within inches of plunging to her death along with him. This marked the end of their affiliation with George Wehner and he fast faded from the group's good graces.

This dissolution of relations was further exacerbated when the *Museum of Religion and Philosophy's* opening was canceled and plans for its future terminated. Several reasons can be surmised as to the museum's failure. Perhaps the fall of the stock market the previous October affected funding for the Roerich Society and mortgage payments on the Master Building became exorbitant. A more compelling reason for the termination of plans for Svetoslav and Natacha's museum was their broken engagement.

By the end of 1930, Helena Roerich issued her final edict regarding the beautiful theosophist her son was planning to marry. In one of her diaries it is revealed she felt Natacha Rambova was the reincarnation of Bathesheba and because of this she was a dangerous influence on Svetoslav's karma.[106] Helena also reiterated her challenge to Alice Bailey and implored Svetoslav to return in India to live with the family. Svetoslav complied, broke his engagement to Natacha and ended all hopes for their museum and their happy theosophical future.

Natacha was furious with Svetie for breaking their engagement and for failing to comply with the promised completion of the *Museum of Religion and Philosophy*. She threatened to sue him for breach of contract. Heeding the voices of reason from Aunt Teresa and her mother, Natacha instead left New York on an ocean voyage sailing for Spain.

What Ever Happened To...

George Wehner

In 1930, George Wehner and Alex Rotov still listed their addresses as the Roerich Master Building at 310 Riverside Drive. Within the next year, George's relationship with Natacha Rambova and Talbot Mundy would end. Mundy would not only reject George, but the entire subject of spiritualism in a dramatic reversal of personal belief. Dawn Allen would write that George Wehner's book, *A Curious Life* was, "the only book she ever threw away." [107]

Despite George's relationship with Talbot Mundy and Natacha Rambova being summarily terminated, he did not yet abandon his activity as medium. He would make a lasting impression on American writer, spiritualist and political activist, William Dudley Pelley. Pelley worked primarily as a journalist but also as a Hollywood screenwriter. He wrote two of Lon Chaney's films, *The Light in the Dark* in 1922 and *The Shock* in 1923, winning two O. Henry Awards. In 1929 his essay, "Seven Minutes in Eternity" published in *The American Magazine* brought him notoriety for his account of a near-death experience. This article put him in contact with George Wehner who conducted many séances with Pelley.

On George's encouragement, Pelley also contemplated recording the messages, or "revelations" delivered in the séances believing this would benefit humanity. Pelley did write extensively about George's abilities in his book titled, *The Dead Are Alive* and included several notable séance occurrences including his conversations with famous authors and screenwriter June Mathis.

In 1933, Pelley founded the Silver Legion of America, a fascist organization which was openly anti-semitic and racist. Pelley was so radical in his fascism he was mentioned in Sinclair Lewis' novel *It Can't Happen Here,* as a precursor to the U.S. fascist movement. In 1942, Pelley was charged with twelve counts of high treason and seditious activity and sentenced to fifteen years in prison.

George distanced himself from Pelley's mention and adopted

several pseudonyms including George Leighton and George Haslett-Wehner, [108] perhaps in an effort to disassociate from Pelley's writings. Despite the advertisement Pelley afforded, George's mediumship with Pelley would mark the end of his career as a psychic. He turned his creative energies to his music and would do so for the remainder of his life.

George composed frenetically and alleged his music was often written by White Cloud. By 1940, he and Alex were living at 156 West 56th Street near Carnegie Hall and in May, an early version of George's piano concerto was broadcast on radio. It was then he hired, "a local New York City arranger, composer, copyist and instrumentalist, Alfred Marion Harned. Harned's assignment was to write out the orchestral parts for George Wehner's piano concerto-for 27 instruments of a symphony orchestra." [109]

George's piano concerto would premiere on August 28, 1941, in the Sculpture Court of the Brooklyn Museum. Greta Lederer, former Viennese pianist, performed as soloist with the New York City Symphony Orchestra, directed by Eugene Plotnikoff.[110]

"Among his (George Wehner's) performed compositions from this period were songs used in concerts by Ernestine Schumann-Heink and Maria Maximovitch; ballets for Katya Sergava and Alex Rotov and symphonic pieces put on by the WNYC Concert Orchestra and the New York City Symphony Orchestra in 1940 and 1941. Throughout the 1940's, Wehner maintained a feverish work pace. He also began to regularly attend the Cantonese Theater of New York. Classical Chinese Theater would have a profound influence on his later works for the stage, such as the opera, *The Mark of King* in 1961." [111]

George and Alex would later move to Brooklyn and there George helped to found the Heights Opera Company. Alex continued to perform as a dancer throughout the 1940's, performing in George Balanchine's *Dream With Music* in 1944, with his last public mention in 1959, when he appeared on an episode of the children's television show, Captain Kangaroo.[112]

George Wehner died at seventy-nine years of age in the Long Island College Hospital in Brooklyn, living at the time at 69 Cranberry Street. It was also reported he married a long time friend, Margreta Overbeck, an artist who designed the Colorado state flag.

Natacha Rambova

Natacha returned to New York from her recovery sail to inform Talbot Mundy and Dawn Allen she was closing her dress shop and moving to Spain. In the course of closing out her business, she would resolve a lawsuit she filed against actress Mae Murray. Her lawsuit pending against Mae Murray alleged the actress owed $1562.00 for an order which included a black coat, a black turban, a necklace and bracelet. According to court records, when the items were delivered to Mae Murray's home in Los Angeles, she refused to pay for them and this instigated Natacha's lawsuit.[113] With this lawsuit resolved in her favor, Natacha completed preparations for her move to Europe. These were expedited in no small measure by a new love interest.

In a rebound from her bitter parting from Svetoslav, Natacha announced she had fallen in love again and this time on the island of Mallorca. Her new love was Spanish nobleman, Alvaro de Ursaiz. Alvaro de Ursaiz was suave, dark-haired, aristocratic and bore a striking resemblance to Rudolph Valentino. With Alvaro, Natacha wasted no time in sealing her relationship and promptly married her Spaniard twice; first in a civil ceremony and then in the Church of San Francisco in Palma, Mallorca. She received the blessings of Alvaro's conservative Catholic family, assumed their surname, "de Ursaiz" and received several of their priceless family heirlooms as wedding gifts.

Natacha Rambova de Ursaiz would never participate in another séance, abandoning her theosophical pursuits and the occult. Her life with Alvaro in her Mediterranean villa became a pastoral and peaceful seaside existence despite the political turmoil in Spain at the time. Natacha left her famous fashion formalities behind and was often seen make-up free, wearing loose trousers, halter tops and espadrilles. She was tan and happy in photos of her life during her first days with Alvaro.

She and Alvaro inspired each other artistically as they launched an ambitious business of restoring villas on the island. They also undertook a complicated project of renovating a local cave system by installing lighting in the passageways. When this project was complete they opened a small restaurant near the entrance which still stands today as, "Ses Coves".[114] They also designed and built their own home high on the rocky cliffs over Mallorca's Cala Fornells. The white stucco, modern villa was christened, "CaNaTacha", local Catalan dialect for "Natacha's Home". CaNaTacha became a Mallorcan retreat for many of Natacha's New York theosophical friends, including Talbot Mundy and his wife Dawn Allen who visited Natacha and Alvaro in 1932.

In January of 1936, Natacha and Alvaro traveled to Egypt where they met with famed Egyptologist, Howard Carter. Natacha's meeting with Carter would change the course of her life as she would recall,

" I felt as if I had at last returned home. The first few days I was there I couldn't stop the tears streaming from my eyes. It was not sadness, but some emotional impact from the past-a returning to a place once loved after too long a time." [115]

War would bring an end to Natacha's life on Mallorca as well as an end to her marriage to Alvaro. Having been too vocal with her opinions about the Spanish Civil War, Natacha's life was deemed in danger and she was advised to flee Mallorca. Secreted aboard a coal freighter, she retreated to the Chateau at Juan les Pins; her port in every storm.

On this arrival, the stress of her exodus from Mallorca and her sorrow at leaving Alvaro caused Natacha to suffer a major heart attack. Alvaro would visit his wife a few times at the chateau during her convalescence before telling her he had fallen in love with another woman. He would eventually ask for an annulment of their marriage based on the grounds she married him with no intention to bear children.

Natacha remained in France during her recovery, traveling only for her academic pursuits. She embraced the subject of Egyptology, studying in London with famed Egyptologist S.R.K. Glanville at University College.[116] In 1939, she returned to Manhattan to further her studies and deliver lectures on dream analysis, astrology and demonstrate palm readings. After a brief sojourn to Arizona, she settled in New York City were she held classes in her apartment with notable New Yorkers as her students. During this academically prolific time for Natacha, she published articles and small books on subjects ranging from dream analysis, Jungian analysis, the symbolism of scarabs and cosmic circuitry and astrology to even posture and physical exercise.

By the mid-1940's Natacha applied for funding from the Bollingen Foundation, seeking a grant to launch an expedition in Egypt's Valley of the Kings where she would study and record the symbols on scarabs. The actual focus of her field work in Egypt would evolve throughout the ensuing years, but she would receive consistent Bollingen funding. With Bollingen grants she completed a transcription of the Tomb of Ramsesses VI as well as a study of the Four Shrines of King Tut Ankh Amon in Cairo.

Natacha's Egyptological pursuits would involve the next twenty years of life. Although she would not spend all of this time in Egypt, her field affiliation with renowned Egyptologist Alexandre Piankoff would result in her collaborating with him on the prestigious, multi-volume, *Egyptian Religious Texts and Representations*. Natacha would act as Piankoff's editor for *The Tomb of Ramsesses VI* as volume one in 1954, *The Shrines of Tut-Ankh-Amon* in 1955 and *Mythological Papyri* in 1957. She would contribute an essay to *Mythological Papyri* and a fourth volume, *Litany of Re* would be dedicated to her.

The most enduring and significant relationship Natacha forged throughout her Egyptological years was with epigrapher, Mark Hasselriis. Natacha hired him as her epigrapher on the Valley of the Kings expedition and he would work with her as her artist, illustrator, secretary, companion and self-avowed disciple for the rest of her life and his. The tall, dark and handsome Mark Hasselriis contributed in great measure to the preservation of the history of Natacha Rambova's post-Valentino legacy. When he was asked if he was in love with Natacha, he replied,

"I wasn't, alas, it was worship of a kind and worship can be wrong because it isn't the best kind of love." [117]

In Natacha's later years, she moved to a New England country estate in New Milford, Connecticut where she lived a reclusive life working on her own life's comprehensive thesis, *The Cosmic Circuit.* Mark Hasselriis would live with her on week-ends and spend much of his time with Natacha both in New York City and in their Connecticut home.

By the early 1960's, Natacha had been diagnosed with schleroderma and the disease took its toll. She experienced increasing difficulties swallowing with Mark Hasselriis recalling that in the last days of her life in Connecticut, Natacha ate only soft-boiled eggs and caviar. After suffering a complete collapse, she was taken to Los Angeles by her aunt and cousin where she died on June 5, 1966 in a nursing home in Pasadena. She spent the last days of her life but a few miles from the final resting place of Rudolph Valentino in Hollywood.

After her death, Mark Hasselriis would spend the rest of his life teaching and lecturing, identifying himself as Natacha Rambova's disciple. He lectured on the subjects of Symbolism, Egyptology, Astrology and the Chakras using "slides from the collection of Natacha Rambova", as illustration. [118] Many of his lectures were held in the grand, yet then dusty parlor of the aging Leslie Grant Scott.

Natacha's ashes were strewn in a forest in Arizona and today her artifacts and collections are housed in various institutions including Yale University, the Utah Museum of Fine Arts, The Philadelphia Museum of Art, The Brooklyn Museum of Art and The Phoenix Art Museum.

What Price Beauty

As Rudolph Valentino's executor, George Ullman endeavored to distribute Natacha's film, *What Price Beauty,* after the star's death as the movie was an asset of the Rudolph Valentino Production Company. Ullman first sought a contract for its distribution with United Artists' President, Joe Schenck. After a few test showings, Schenck informed George he had no interest in the film. George then went to the Pathé Company where he negotiated a contract for their worldwide distribution of the film.

In *The Exhibitor's Trade Review,* August 1925, it is reported Natacha and Ullman were in New York to "arrange a release" of the movie. But it would not be until 1928, that the film would be shown publicly. Pathé released the film to a limited audience with notices appearing in trade publications. The film's producer is cited as S. George Ullman with its release date as January 28, 1928 and the final length of the film as 4000 feet.

With meager audience interest in the film, Pathé dropped the project. This left George Ullman fighting unsuccessfully for Pathé's return of the film's original negative. He was finally informed the negative had been destroyed. Natacha's movie, *What Price Beauty* is a lost film and exists today only as movie stills, articles and advertisement.

R.T. M. Scott

R.T.M. Scott would achieve more success in 1935 when his action novel, *The Spider* was produced as a popular weekly radio show. His son, R.T. M. Scott, Junior, followed in his father's literary footsteps by working at *Popular Publications*. He was acting editor of the *True Mystic Magazine* in November 1938 and it was R.T.M. Jr. who published George Wehner's article "*The Valentino Death Prophecy*".

In the February 17, 18 and 19th, 1931, issues of the Hearst Press Syndicate, three notable articles by R.T.M. Scott were featured. These articles seemed to authenticate the ability to communicate with the astral, or mahatma Rudolph Valentino.

Scott, then chairman of the New York division of the American Society for Psychical Research wrote the articles as an account of how actress Ruth Roland conversed with Valentino during a séance conducted by George Wehner. She presented a series of questions and believed she received her answers from the discarnate Rudy. [119]

R.T.M. Scott Junior was killed during World War Two, and his father would pass away in 1966 in New York at the age of eighty-three.

Leslie Grant Scott

Leslie Grant Scott would author one publication, *Dying as a Liberation of Consciousness* published in 1931 in the journal for the American Society for Psychical Research. She outlived her husband R.T.M. and resided in their opulent home in New York the rest of her life. Mark Hasselriis befriended Leslie and wrote that she analyzed dreams as an "enthusiastic Jungian who also gave Rorschach tests." [120] Hasselriis would deliver a series of lectures in her parlor in the early 1970's.

Leslie Scott's actual date of death is unknown but as Mark Hasselriis visited her some years after R.T.M.'s death in 1966, it is assumed she lived into the 1970's and well into her eighties.

Talbot Mundy

Talbot Mundy would renounce all interest in the occult and sell the rights to some of his more popular books to movie studios including his best-selling novels *The Winds of the World* and *King of Khyber Rifles*. Mundy wrote forty-seven novels, one hundred and thirty novelettes or short stories and twenty-three non-fiction articles which were published in magazines such as *Adventure, Cavalier* and *Argosy*.

He married five times, with Dawn Allen being his fifth wife. His biographer, Brian Taves states Mundy was, "engaged in a lifelong discourse on philosophy and religion, including Eastern ideas on subjects like **karma** and **reincarnation** which would later be popularized by the New Age movement."[121] His **body of work survives** to enjoy continued appreciation.

Talbot Mundy died in August 1940 at sixty-one years of age.

Svetoslav Roerich

Svetoslav Roerich lived the remainder of his life in India, recognized as a celebrated artist. In 1936-1937, a first exhibition of his art was held at the State Exhibition of the United Provinces in Lucknow. Continuous exhibitions of his work were organized and in 1941, Svetoslav was commissioned to paint the first of several official portraits he would complete of India's Prime Minister, Jawaharlal Nehru. In 1945, he married Indian film star, Devika Rani Chaudhuri, known as Devika Rani. At the time she was acting administrator of the film studio, "Bombay Talkies".

After their marriage, Svetoslav and Devika lived outside of Bangalore on a large estate they christened, "Tataguni." In addition to collecting local folk items and studying flora, Svetoslav continued to be a prolific artist with his paintings being showcased throughout India, Europe and Russia. In 1960, a comprehensive retrospective of his work was held in Delhi. That same year Svetoslav returned to Russia for an exhibition of his art in the State Pushkin Museum of Fine Arts in Moscow.

Svetoslav Roerich died at the age of eighty-eight in 1993 and is buried on his estate in Bangalore. [122]

Alice Bailey

Alice Bailey and her husband Foster Bailey founded the Lucis Trust in 1922, which is still in existence. The primary activity of the Lucis trust is the promotion and management of the Arcane School. Alice and Foster Bailey also established a publishing company to publish Alice's books. She died in 1949 at sixty-nine years of age.

Aunt Teresa Werner

Aunt Teresa lived the remainder of her life in Los Angeles. At the request of Valentino's estate executor, George Ullman, she would returned to Los Angeles in November of 1926, to guard her interests in Valentino's estate. Teresa Werner would pass away at seventy-six years of age in 1941.

Muzzie Hudnut

Before the German invasion of France in 1939, Muzzie received warning of the Nazi advance while at the chateau. She acted quickly by having her collection of antiques and treasures crated and shipped to New York. Upon her return to New York and throughout the 1940's, she bequeathed her entire collection to the University of Utah. The contribution was extensive and in order to accommodate the tapestries, oil paintings, Louis XVI furniture, artifacts and jewelry, the university dedicated a floor in a campus building as the Hudnut Gallery which opened on May 6, 1951. The collection has since been relocated and is now housed in the Utah Museum of Fine Arts. Muzzie died in September of 1957. [123]

George Wehner's monkey

George Wehner's monkey appears to have survived at least two years in Manhattan. A photograph of Talbot Mundy holding the monkey reveals the little beast was doing well when Mundy arrived in New York in the summer of 1928.

Cousin Cassio

As I neared completion of this book, I received a surprising article from an archivist in London. The article appeared in *The Exhibitor's Herald and Moving Picture World* on August 25, 1928 and included an advertisement for a movie titled, *Who Am I?* starring Natacha Rambova and an actor, Cassio. I knew there was no mention of this film in Natacha's filmography and could scarcely believe what I was reading. Yet there it was; an image of Natacha Rambova seated left, facing forward and to her left stood an actor in mid conversation with a caption reading,

"Right: Star and feminine lead in a feature-length comedy made by the Prince Film Producing Company. Cassio, Italian comedian, heads the cast of *Who Am I?* in which he is supported by Natacha Rambova, widow of Valentino, who is shown with Cassio here. The picture is the first of a series being directed by John L. McCutcheon."

An immediate search of "Rambova and Cassio" in newspaper archives revealed a few more mentions in which Cassio was billed as the "The European Charlie Chaplin", "Comedy Star of International Fame" and "A Cousin of Rudolph Valentino". [124] It was alleged he was sponsored in America by an ex-official of the Italian government, Joseph Cassisi.[125] In one article Cassio was referred to as an Italian Cavaliere; a prestigious honor bestowed on notable Italians by the King of Italy, then King Vittorio Emanuele III.

These articles advertising the movie, *Who Am I?* shared more thrilling news. Natacha Rambova was scheduled to appear in a second film, a "talkie" titled, *That's Nothing* with Cassio and his Prince Film Producing Company of 1480 Broadway at 42nd Street, New York City [126] I had to wonder; did Natacha Rambova make a talking film? Was there actually a recording of her voice?

My first reaction to news of this film was to consider its timing rather mystifying. At the time of its release in the summer of 1928,

Natacha Rambova was involved in serious endeavors and had gone down her many other paths. That summer she granted several interviews to announce her dress shop was such a success she was expanding into the wholesale market. She was also involved with both the Theosophical Society and the Roerich Society and enjoying the early days of her love affair with Svetoslav Roerich. She had not appeared in a movie in three years and her few stage appearances since that time were nothing to write home about. So I wondered how she came to appear in Cassio's, *Who Am I*? And who was Cassio?

I set out to learn all I possibly could about Cassio and began by contacting the Cineteca di Bologna in Italy; a prestigious European film library. They responded to my request for information by saying they had nothing in their archives regarding Cassio's career in Italy or in Europe. They did, however, find references to his American films. The most significant data learned from the Cineteca di Bologna was that Cassio's birth name was "Domenico Nicassio".

An online search of ship manifests revealed Domenico Nicassio's arrival in New York aboard the vessel "Giuseppe Verdi" arriving on September 8, 1922 from Naples. He was then twenty-five years old and his occupation listed as "Artist". His birthplace was recorded as Canneto di Bari, his father as Gennaro Nicassio and mother as Vita Gaetana Cesarea Guglielmi.

At this point in my Cassio research, the London archivist forwarded a link to the Sixth-Annual Silent Film Identification Workshop investigating "Mostly-Lost Films", sponsored by the Library of Congress in June of 2017 and held in Culpeper, Virginia at the Packard Campus for Audio Visual Conservation. One of the film historians participating in the event was Dr. Robert J. Kiss who delivered a lecture titled, "Silent Film's Most Forgotten Star? The Lost Italian-American Laughter of Cassio."

I contacted Dr. Kiss and he graciously shared his Cassio research with me including the images he used in his lecture and a transcript of his speech. Cassio's identity and the history of Natacha Rambova's last and lost movie began to take shape.

Dr. Kiss' lecture focused on the silent genre he refers to as, "...the fly-by-night world of poverty-row, silent comedy films shot in and around New York City during the 1920's." [127] His particular attention was paid to "...East Coast Italian-American poverty row comedies produced between 1923-1929." [128]

According to Dr. Kiss, Domenico Nicassio changed his name to Cassio after getting the idea from the "Cassio Film Company" which was owned and operated in New York City by his cousin Trifone Nicassio and Trifone's father Vittore.

Cassio began his career in America as a member of a vaudeville act performing as the "DeRosa's" and it was there he met his wife, Valentina in 1925. He soon collaborated with his cousin Trifone and Uncle Vittore to learn the business of comedy film making. In this endeavor he would establish his own business, the Boheme Film Company and partner with Caterina Avella.

Caterina Avella not only acted in Cassio's films, she also wrote his screenplays. The short comedic films produced by Cassio's Boheme Film Company and written by Avella addressed themes of interest to the Italian immigrant population such as proficiency in English and Americanization in general.

By the beginning of 1928, Cassio changed the name of his company to the Prince Film Producing Company. He announced he was again collaborating with actress and screenplay writer, Caterina Avella on his first full-feature movie titled, *Who Am I?* which was scheduled to be filmed at the Pathé Manhattan Studios. The bigger news was that *Who Am I?* would feature an appearance by none other than Natacha Rambova.

In Cassio's promotional material for this film, he made a few additions to his public profile. In advance of his screen appearance with Natacha Rambova, Cassio advertised himself as "Domenico Cassio Guglielmi" and alleged he was "Rudolph 'Guglielmi' Valentino's cousin". His personal promos included the titles of "Cav." an abbreviation of "Cavaliere" and "U Barese", which is the Italian Region of Puglia slang expression meaning "The man from Bari". [129]

In his lecture, Dr. Kiss points out that although Cassio's mother's surname was Guglielmi, as was Valentino's, and although Cassio came from a city only thirty miles from Valentino's birthplace of Castellaneta, he was unable to find any connection between the two men.

At this point in my research, I contacted noted Valentino historian and researcher Professor Aurelio Miccoli; a native of

Castellaneta, in the Region of Puglia and Valentino's birthplace. While researching his book on Rudolph Valentino's childhood, *The Infancy of the Myth*, he became familiarized with local archives, genealogical resources and was locally renown as a scholar studying the history of Rudolph Valentino's family. Professor Miccoli agreed to investigate any connection between Cassio and Rudolph Valentino. Was there a family connection which might explain why Natacha Rambova would agree to appear in Cassio's film? Did Rudolph Valentino have a cousin producing Italian-American comedy films in New York in the 1920's?

Professor Miccoli first located Cassio's birth certificate and his parent's marriage certificate in the archives of the city of Adelfia; a city created in 1927 through the unification of two small cities, Canneto and Montrone. Cassio's registry entries revealed he was born in Canneto on November 28, 1897, with his mother being Vita Gaetana Cesarea Guglielmi, his father Gennaro Nicassio and his brother christened Vincenzo.

Professor Miccoli was remarkably successful in his search for existing family members in the region. Through his connections with local historians, an interview was arranged between Professsor Miccoli and Cassio's great-nephew, a lawyer and amateur actor, Avv.(Italian prefix for lawyer) Giovanni Monteleone of Adelfia.

Giovanni Monteleone shared his family's history in regards to his relative Domenico Nicassio, "Cassio" with Professor Miccoli. As Cassio's great-nephew, his maternal grandfather was Cassio's brother Vincenzo, his great-grandmother was Vita Gaetana Cesarea Guglielmi; a relative of Valentino's father, Giovanni Guglielmi. During the interview, Mr. Monteleone recalled how his mother attributed their artistic interests as a family to their famous relative Rudolph Valentino. "We are all artists like Valentino!" she often said to her son, Giovanni.

During Professor Miccoli's interview with Mr. Monteleone, he was invited to photograph a collection of framed images of Cassio's American film career which were prominently displayed in the Monteleone home. Many family stories were shared about their artistic and colorful relative, Cassio, including his chronological history and the mention of his sensibility for beautiful women.

Through his connection with Giovanni Monteleone, Professor Miccoli confirmed a family connection between Cassio and Rudolph Valentino. Yet this presented further questions for me; did Rudolph Valentino know Domenico Nicassio in Italy? Had they met in New

York when Cassio was performing in his vaudeville act, the "DeRosa's"? When did Natacha Rambova first meet Cassio?

From the timelines of both Rudolph Valentino and Cassio's lives, it can be surmised that they could have met in New York after 1923 as they were both living in the city at the time. It is not known whether they were in contact in Italy before Valentino left for America in 1913. With only a two year age difference between the two young Guglielmis, it is possible that as teen-agers they spent time together. With a connection between the two men presented, I was intrigued to know more about Rambova's last movie.

In Dr. Kiss' speech, he surmises the plot of *Who Am I?* as the script has not been located to date. He constructed the basic plotline from the scant press coverage for the film and the few surviving images. The story line appears to have been centered around Cassio's character having amnesia and his confusion over whether his wife was a plain woman, played by Camille Renault [130] or Natacha Rambova, "the woman who always wore the pearls."

Perhaps Cassio was inspired to use the subject of amnesia in the film's script by reading the headlines in Italian-American newspapers at the time. In Italy in 1927, the high profile case of Bruneri and Canella was then holding audiences rapt. Emotions about the case ran high with Italian-American populations sharply divided over the gripping drama.

The case involved the story of a man named Canella, a World War One amnesia victim who wandered lost in Northern Italy and an impostor, Bruneri, who came forward to assume Canella's identity. The impostor Bruneri resembled Canella and would so successfully convince Canella's wife he was her lost husband, she would bear three children with him. Despite a court ruling Bruneri to be a total fraud, Canella's wife was not convinced and left for Brazil with the man she believed to be her husband, the bandit Bruneri. Did the story on all the front pages of Italian-American newspapers at the time inspire Cassio's film, *Who Am I?*

On July 2, 1928, Cassio began distributing his first full-length movie, *Who Am I?* by having it shown in East Coast Italian-American theaters. He appeared confidant in having Natacha Rambova star in the film and made an announcement on August 22, 1928, revealing his new invention which he called, "Moviesound".

"A new talking device will be used by the Prince Film Producing Company for a series of features starring Cassio, Italian-American comedian and cousin of Rudolph Valentino.

It is known as 'Moviesound' and is a brand new patent different from those now on the market. Cassio has completed his first independent picture, *Who Am I?* and will make *That's Nothing* a talking picture as his second feature-length comedy." [131]

However, Cassio struggled to secure a broad audience for *Who Am I?* With box-office returns meager, Cassio lost money on its release and his Prince Films Producing Company soon went bankrupt. There was no funding for his Moviesound device or to invest in his next film *That's Nothing,* a talkie slated to star Natacha Rambova.

By August of 1929, Cassio was unable to pay the rent at the Lloyd's Film Storage Facility and all twenty reels of his footage were sold at auction. *Who Am I?* appears to have then disappeared. Prince Film Producing Company and Cassio's career as a film producer folded. Cassio returned to the vaudeville circuit but would surface one year later in Dayton, Ohio.

According to local Dayton newspapers in September of 1930, "Cavaliere Cassio" announced he would be opening the Aum European Studios in Dayton on October fifteenth. His studio would offer a broad curriculum including, "Dramatic Courses, Taught for Opera, Drama, Talkies, Stage and Screen." [132] Cassio's press release promoted himself as Rudolph Valentino's cousin and states he spent the previous two years as the director of the Paramount Conservatory of Art in New York. [133]

Cassio's school of operatic instruction announced one of his "Italian artist teachers" as Carla Castellani. Carla Castellani was a well-known soprano then singing in La Scala in Milan and would not visit the United States until the fall of 1946 when she made her American debut touring the country singing in *Tosca.*[134] It appears Cassio's Aum European Studios never realized.

According to his great-nephew, Giovanni Monteleone, at that

time Cassio returned to his home town in southern Italy with his wife and young son Gennaro. It was then he organized many dramatic productions and stage shows in the Region of Puglia which were well received.

In 1935, a ship's manifest lists Cassio, "Domenico Nicassio" and his wife Valentina and son Gennaro as passengers arriving in New York City. In September of 1939 Cassio and his wife would divorce and he moved to Providence, Rhode Island to find work as an actor.

Dr. Kiss reports that after a stage performance in Providence, Rhode Island on April 19, 1940, Cassio collapsed and died of a heart attack at forty-two years old. Perhaps a mystery exists in this account as a United States Census worker recorded a Domenico Nicassio, "Actor" as a lodger at 84 Broadway in Providence on April 24, 1940. [135]

The answer to my question of why Natacha Rambova appeared in Cassio's one full-length movie was found in a small mention in the French publication, *Cine Comoedia*. It was there reported she made the film because she and Rudolph Valentino promised Cassio they would help him.[136] The article was titled, "A Family Affair" and read in its entirety:

"Cassio, cousin of Rudolph Valentino, has remained on excellent terms with Natacha Rambova. The wife of the celebrated artist had promised Cassio that she would not to lose sight of him and even, on occasion, offered to help him. This was not a promise in the air, since we learn that Cassio will make two films including one scheduled to be a talkie. Cassio, on the screen, will remain Cassio. This is a wise decision and even heroic, because it is certain that Valentino's name has tempted him quite often. But this is due to the fact that Valentino's brother, Alberto, comes to Hollywood to make a sensational debut in the film titled, *Tropic Madness*. Alberto, himself, will be called Valentino, whose real name, like his brother, was Guglielmi. Let us wish him to have, as we say, backbone, because although it's a wonderful inheritance, it appears a heavy name to bear."

Dr. Kiss poses the question; if Cassio was a Guglielmi relative why did he not make mention of this earlier when Valentino died in 1926. This could be explained as Cassio had no audience to explain this to at that time. Yet this presents another question; was Valentino's brother, Alberto Guglielmi who was then in Hollywood pursuing his own movie career, in contact with Cassio?

In the late 1920's, Alberto Guglielmi was in the throes of aggressively policing his deceased brother Rudolph's legacy and certainly would have protested the use of his brother's name if the connection was false. Perhaps Alberto Guglielmi hoped his relative's Prince Film Producing Company would offer him screen roles.

For after two years attempting to replace his brother Rudolph on screen, Alberto Guglielmi appeared in but one movie, *Tropic Madness* which opened in December of 1928. Was there an affiliation between Cassio and Alberto Guglielmi? Perhaps so. For coincidentally, while Cassio was promoting *Who Am I?*, an Alberto Production Company was also producing Italian-American short films.

Could Cassio's lost reels of footage of *Who Am I?*, sold at auction in 1929, still exist in some archive? Will Natacha Rambova's last screen appearance be found; a movie she made as a generous gesture to a cousin of her lost love Rudolph?

The photograph of the cast of *Who Am I?*, which Giovanni Monteleone so generously shared for inclusion in this book, reveals a cordial gathering of actors, cameraman and director. Natacha Rambova sits demurely bestowing a supportive glance at Cassio, the man who cast her in this final screen role as the woman who always wore pearls. Her appearance in this lost film stands as a touching footnote to her love for Rudolph and a definitive statement as to the familial connection between Rudolph Valentino and "Cassio"; Cavaliere, U Barese.

The End Notes

1 George Ullman, *The S. George Ullman Memoir,* p. 48.
2 Herb Howe, "Her Years As Valentino's Wife", *The New Movie Magazine,* December 1929-May 1930.
3 Ibid.
4 Ibid.
5 Irving Schulman, *Valentino,* p. 437.
6 MacFadden would also publish, *How To Keep Fit* by Valentino in 1923.
7 Evelyn Zumaya, *Affairs Valentino,* p. 168-169.
8 Ullman, *The S. George Ullman Memoir,* p. 63.
9 Natacha Rambova, *Rudy: An Intimate Portrait of Rudolph Valentino by His Wife Natacha Rambova,* p. 139.
10 Michael Morris interview notes and the Madam Valentino Archive.
11 *Exhibtor's Trade Review,* August 1925.
12 "Affections Switch From Sheik to Peke, Valentino to Aid Divorce", *Los Angeles Times,* November 14, 1925.
13 Ibid.
14 *International Newsreel Photo & Press Release,* August 24, 1925.
15 Ullman, *The S. George Ullman Memoir,* p. 192-193.
16 "Mrs. Valentino to Appear in F.B.O. Film." *Moving Picture World,* November-December, 1925.
17 *Moving Picture World,* January 16, 1926.
18 *The Daily News,* New York, New York, November 14, 1925.
19 "Miss Rambova Desires That the World Forget She Was Valentino's Wife." *Santa Ana Register,* January 20, 1926.
20 George Wehner, *A Curious Life,*1929.
21 "Rambova Picture Titled, When Love Grows Cold." *Exhibitor's Herald,* December 15, 1925.
22 *When Love Grows Cold.* A review by William Campbell.
23 "Faith Cited in Row Over Spirit Talk", *The Los Angeles Times,* December 1, 1926.
24 Robert L. Harned interviews and research notes.
25 Ibid.
26 Wehner, *A Curious Life.*
27 Ibid.
28 Howe, "Her Years as Valentino's Wife".
29 Ibid.
30 Wehner, *A Curious Life,* p. 111-115.
31 Ibid., p.18.
32 Michael Morris and Evelyn Zumaya, *Beyond Valentino,* p. 12-13.
33 Robert L. Harned interviews.
34 Mark Hasselriis letter to Michael Morris in the Madam Valentino Archive.
35 Ibid.
36 Rambova, *Rudy, An Intimate Portrait of Rudolph Valentino.* p. 139.
37 *Santa Ana Register,* January 20, 1926.
38 "Mrs. Valentino is at Hartford Theater", *The Hartford Courant,* January 10, 1926.
39 *A Curious Life,* p.348.
40 "La Rampe au Cinema", *La Rampe,* (the Limelight), Paris, May 15, 1926.

Gallica Archive.

41 Ibid., p.363.
42 Ibid., p.367.
43 Appendix IV, "Gift of Art Treasure From Mrs. Winifred K. Hudnut", The Madam Valentino Archive.
44 Ibid.
45 Wehner, "The Valentino Death Prophecy", *True Mystic Science Magazine*, November 1938.
46 Ibid.
47 Ibid.
48 The account of the séance events are taken from *A Curious Life,* by George Wehner.
49 Ibid.
50 Ibid.
51 Ibid.
52 Ibid.
53 Ibid.
54 Ibid.
55 "Sheik's Shade Waits Cue", *Los Angeles Times*, November 26, 1926.
56 "Valentino's Spirit Life Told by Miss Hudnut", *Washington Post,* November 26, 1926.
57 "Astral Rudy Writing a Book Through Her Says Ex-Wife", *New York Daily News*, November 27, 1926.
58 "Hears from 'Rudy' Wife Says; Houdini's Widow Scouts Idea", *The Bridgeport Telegram*, November 30, 1926.
59 Rambova, *Rudy, An Intimate Portrait.*
60 Wallace Reid, silent film actor, died at thirty-one years of age after suffering from an addiction to morphine.
61 Vernon Castle, a dancer who would die at thirty-one years of age while flying.
62 Harold Lockwood was a silent era leading man who would also die at age thirty-one.
63 Olive Thomas was a silent era actress who would die of an accidental poisoning at age twenty-five.
64 Jimmy Quirk was the editor of *Photoplay* magazine.
65 Bobby Herron was a film star who would commit suicide at age twenty-seven.
66 Charles Frohman was a theatrical producer and Clyde Fitch a playwright.
67 Curley Stecker was an animal trainer in Hollywood.
68 "What No Movies in Heaven?" *New York Daily News, Sunday News Section*, December 5, 1926.
69 Ibid.
70 "Hears From 'Rudy' Wife Says; Houdini's Widow Scouts Idea", *The Bridgeport Telegram*, Bridgeport, Connecticut, November 30, 1926.
71 "Faith Cited in Row Over Spirit Talk." *Los Angeles Daily Times,* December 1, 1926.
72 Ibid.
73 Ann Herr, "Over the Teacups", *The Reading Times,* Reading, Pennsylvania, November 30, 1926.

74 https://en.wikipedia.org/wiki/Composograph
75 Frederick James Smith, "Does Rudy Speak From the Beyond?" *Photoplay Magazine*, February 1927.
76 Frank Mallen, *Sauce for the Gander,* p. 105.
77 Bob Stepno, "The Evening Graphic's Tabloid Reality". www.stepno.com.
78 Mallen, *Sauce for the Gander.*
79 Ibid.
80 Wehner, *A Curious Life,* p. 376.
81 *Photoplay* magazine, February 1927, p. 38, 39 and 104.
82 "Natacha Rambova Attends", *The Evening News*, Wilkes Barre, PA, April 22, 1927.
83 Morris. *Madam Valentino.*
84 "Her Years as Valentino's Wife", *The Moving Picture World.*
85 Morris & Zumaya, *Beyond Valentino.*
86 Michael Morris interview with Ann Wollen.
87 Mark Hasselriis correspondence with Michael Morris, November, 7, 1986.
88 https://www.lucistrust.org/arcane_school
89 Ibid.
90 Robert L. Harned interviews.
91 Michael Morris writes in *Madam Valentino*, "... he (George Wehner) left the United States for a year-long excursion through Europe with his homosexual lover." p. 191.
92 Morris, *Madam Valentino*, p. 193.
93 Brian Taves, *Talbot Mundy, Philosopher of Adventure, a Critical Biography.*
94 Wehner, *A Curious Life*, p. 386.
95 "Step Out, Wear Color, Express Yourself", *Dayton Daily News*, Dayton Ohio, August 12, 1928.
96 Taves, *Talbot Mundy*, p. 169.
97 Morris, *Madam Valentino*, p. 196.
98 Ibid., p. 171.
99 Ibid.
100 *Paris-Soir,* June, 21, 1929. Gallica Archive.
101 "Two Prima Donnas..." *Chicago Tribune,* July 28, 1929. "American Opera in Paris", *Chicago Tribune*, May 12, 1929. "American Opera Company Makes Hit in Paris", *The Akron Beacon Journal,* June 20, 1929. "Widow of Valentino Scorns Paris Modes", *Lansing State Journal,* July 26, 1929.
102 "Roerich Museum Elects", *New York Times,* August 18, 1929.
103 Taves, p. 175.
104 Ibid.
105 Ibid. p. 175-176.
106 *Agni Yogi Forum*, August-September 2002.
107 Taves, p. 176.
108 World Cat archives, George Wehner, "Abstract".
109 Harned, *Sally Phipps, Silent Film Star, by Her Son Robert L. Harned*, p. 162.
110 *The Brooklyn Daily Eagle,* August 28, 1941.
111 The New York Public Library, Music Division, "George Wehner".
112 Barbara Naomi Cohen-Stratyner, *Biographical Dictionary of Dance,* p. 774-775.

113 "Valentino's Widow Sues Mae Murray", *Exhibitor's Review & Motion Picture Today*, February 28, 1930.

114 Morris & Zumaya, *Beyond Valentino*, p. 325.

115 Letter from Natacha Rambova to Ann Wollen, March 1, 1965, The Madam Valentino Archive.

116 *Beyond Valentino*, p. 292.

117 Mark Hasselriis letter to Michael Morris, Madam Valentino Archive.

118 *The Long Island Advance*, December 9, 1976, p. 27.

119 Irving Schulman, *Valentino*.

120 Hasselriis correspondence with Michael Morris, August 6, 1987.

121 Taves, p.1

122 *Beyond Valentino*, p. 491.

123 Madam Valentino Archive. Utah Museum correspondence files.

124 Ibid.

125 *New York Daily News*, June 26, 1928.

126 *The Exhibitor's Herald and Moving Picture World*, August 25, 1928.

127 Transcript of lecture by Dr. Robert James Kiss.

128 Ibid.

129 *Film Daily*, March 2, 1927 and *Motion Pictures*, February 18, 1927.

130 Camille Renault was an actress who promoted herself as being French but she was from Kokomo, Indiana.

131 *Exhibtor's Daily Review*, archive.

132 Aum European Studios advertisement, *Dayton Daily News*, Sept. 21, 1930.

133 "Will Have Direction of Aum European Studio Here", *Dayton Daily News* September 28, 1930.

134 , "Opera Schedule", *Chicago Tribune*, October 13, 1946 and October 20, 1946.

135 The Sixteenth Census of the United States, 1940.

136 *Cine-Comoedia*, February 14, 1929. Original French: "Affaires de Famille - Cassio, cousin de Rudolph Valentino, était demeuré en excellents termes avec Natacha Rambova. Celle qui fut la fame du célèbre artiste avait promis à Cassio de ne pas le perdre de vue et même, à l'occasion, de l'aider. Ce n'atait pas là promesses en l'air, puisque nous apprenons que Cassio doit débuter prochainement dans deux films dont l'un serà parlant. Cassio, à l'écran, restera Cassio. Voilà une résolution sage qui peut- être même héroïque, car il est certain que le nom de Valentino a dû le tenter bien souvent. Mais ceci s'explique du fait que le frère de Valentino, Albert, vient da faire, à Hollywood, des debuts sensationnnels dans le film intitulé: La Folie des Tropiques. Albert, lui, s'appellera naturellement Valentino, comme son frère, dont le vrai nom, d'ailleurs, était Guglielmi. Souhaitons-lui d'avoir, comme on le dit, les reins solides évidemment un héritage merveilleux, mais combien lourd à porter!"

The Album

2. Claude Falls Wright

3. Helena Petrovna Blavatsky

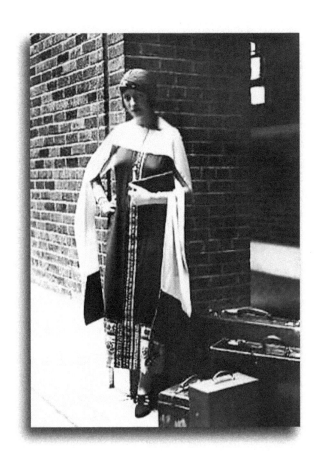

4. Natacha Rambova leaving Hollywood forever in
August of 1925.

5. Natacha Rambova in August of 1925.

6. Natacha's Aunt Teresa Werner & Rudolph Valentino's
manager, George Ullman's wife, Beatrice. 1926.

7. Natacha Rambova with her mother, Winifred Hudnut,
"Muzzie".

8. George Benjamin Wehner.

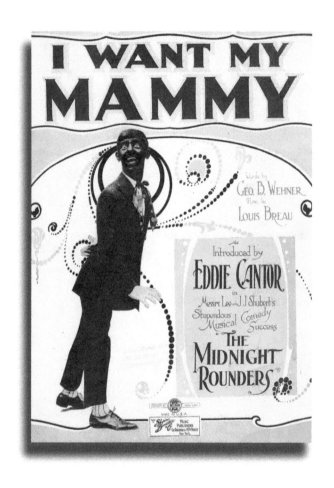

9. George Wehner's hit song, "I Want My Mammy".

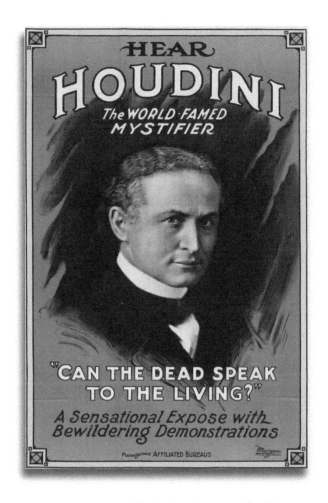

10. Harry Houdini advertisement for his
"Bewildering Demonstrations".

11. Magician Harry Houdini says no.

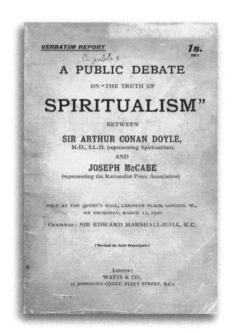

12. The public spiritualism debate rages.

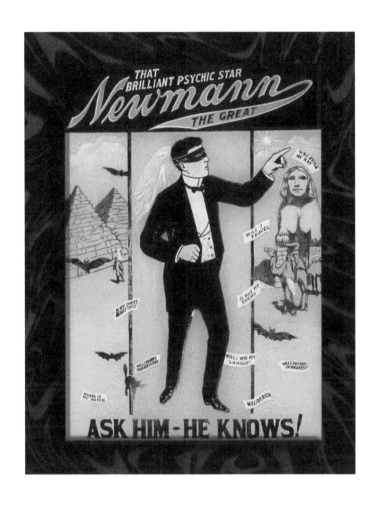

13. Egyptian Influence.

14. *When Love Grows Cold*, sheet music.

HARRY O. HOYT
Director
"THE LOST WORLD"

Recently Completed
NATACHA RAMBOVA
(Mrs. Rudolph Valentino)
"When Love Grows Cold"

15. Harry O. Hoyt, director of *When Love Grows Cold.*

16. Caption reads - "Six of the mannequins in *When Love Grows Cold,* the F.B.O. Gold Bond production starring Natacha Rambova, until recently the wife of Rudolph Valentino".

163

17. *When Love Grows Cold* - Natacha Rambova
with Clive Brook.

18. Clive Brook & Natacha Rambova.

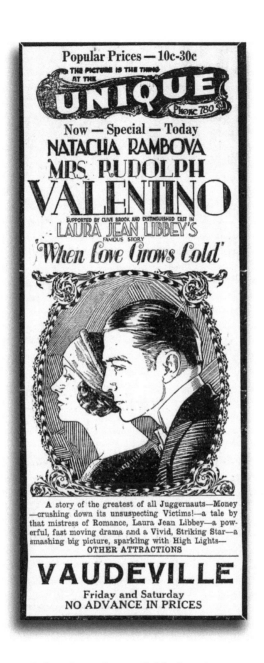

19. *When Love Grows Cold* advertisement.

20. Clive Brook, Russell Griffin & Natacha Rambova in *When Love Grows Cold.*

21. *When Love Grows Cold,* Sam Hardy with Natacha Rambova.

22. Promotional still from *When Love Grows Cold.*

23. Promotional still from *When Love Grows Cold.*

24. Rudolph Valentino & Manuel Reachi arrive in Paris, 1925.

25. Rudolph Valentino receives top billing in Natacha Rambova's film debug.

26. Aunt Elsie DeWolfe.

27. Those striped awnings on a Villa Trianon terrace.

28. The Chateau Juan les Pins, 2017.

29. The Casino & Promenade at Juan les Pins, early 1930's.

30. Juan les Pins harbor.

31. Advertising Juan les Pins.

32-33. The French Riviera socialites & avant guarde friends - Mrs. Cora Brown Potter (above) & Loie Fuller (below) 1926.

34. Rudolph Valentino, Natacha Rambova & the doberman Kabar on the Court of Palms at the Chateau, Juan les Pins, 1923.

35. Paja Jovanović - Paul Ivanovitch, resident artist at the Hudnut chateau, 1926.

36. Helena Petrovna Blavatsky, portrait by Paul Ivanovitch.

37. Richard Hudnut heat lamp perfume atomizer.

38. Foyer of the Chateau.

39. The Chateau library.

40. A Chateau sitting room

41. Natacha Rambova's bedroom at the chateau.

42. Natacha Rambova in Paris

43. Alice Bailey

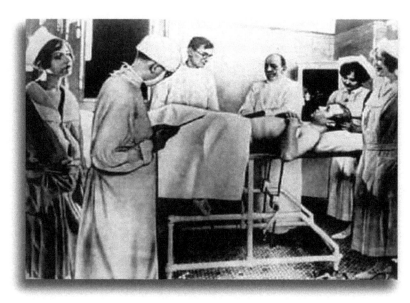

44.-45. *The New York Evening Graphic's* composograph depictions of Rudolph Valentino in heaven with Enrico Caruso and prior to surgery.

46. *The New York Evening Graphic's* composograph as "Revelations" illustration.

46a. *The New York Evening Graphic's* composograph as illustration of Rudolph Valentino meeting Helena Blavatsky in the after life.

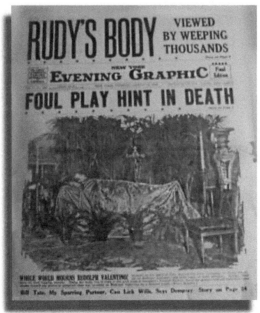

47. - 48. Publisher Bernarr MacFadden & a copy of one of his Rudolph
Valentino composographs.

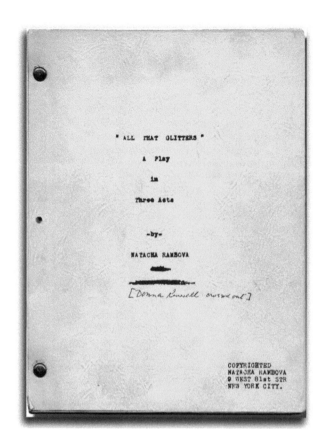

49. Natacha Rambova's screenplay, "All That Glitters".

50. Natacha Rambova @ 1927.

51. Natacha begins to change her Hollywood style.

52. Adapting a more academic image.

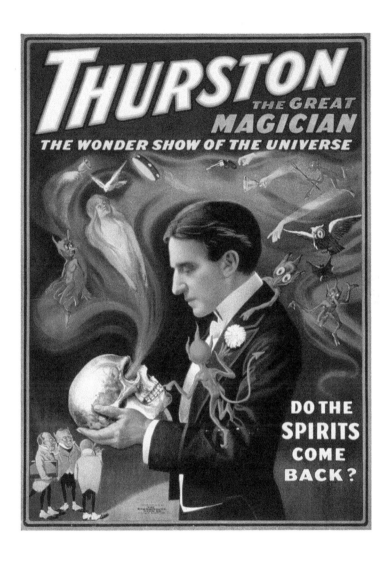

53. The magicians exploited the subject and the spiritualists believed it.
A grieving world sought the answer.

54. - 55. George Wehner (left) and Alex Rotov (right)

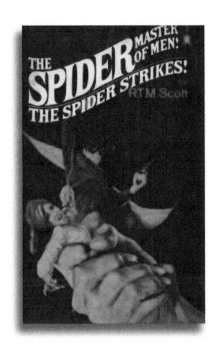

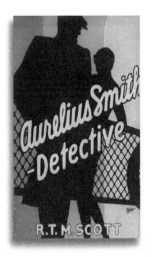

56. R.T.M. Scott & his two most successful novels.

57. Talbot Mundy.

58. Talbot Mundy with George Wehner's Monkey.

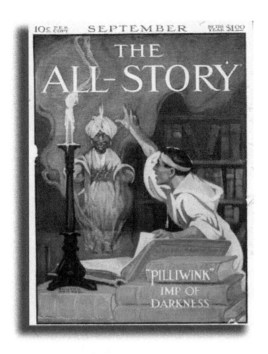

59. Two of Talbot Mundy's finest works in short story and in novel
format.

60.- 61. Svetoslav Roerich (above) and the Roerich family (below).
Nicholas Roerich, Helena Roerich, George and Svetoslav (left to right)

194

62.- 63. Svetoslav Roerich in India & one of his sketches of Natacha.

64. Natacha modeling Paul Poiret.

65. 310 Riverside Drive, Manhattan, The Roerich Master Building.

66. - 67. Svetoslav Roerich sketches Natacha Rambova.

68. Pencil sketches by Natacha Rambova.

69. Señor Alvaro de Ursaiz on the
Juan les Pins Court of Palms.

70. Natacha Rambova de Ursaiz with Tony on her right and Bimbo on
her left, Mallorca.

71. Rudolph Valentino covers *Fate Magazine* in March of 1956.

72. *True Mystic Science Magazine*, November 1938, "The Valentino Death Prophecy" included in this issue.

73. Natacha Rambova in her forties.

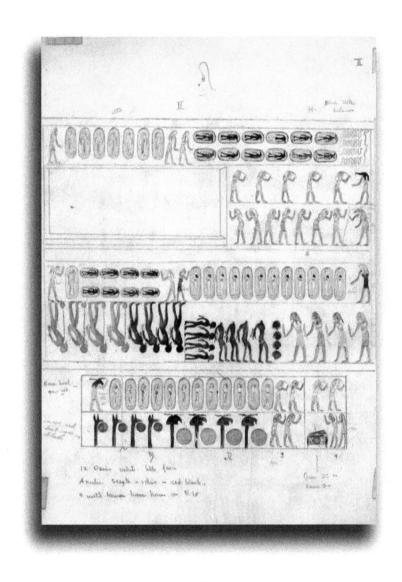

74.
Natacha Rambova's handwritten field notations, *The Book of Caverns*
from the tomb of Ramesses VI.

75. Cassio's advertisement for his Prince Film Producing Company,
Incorporated.

76. Comedy Star of International Fame, "Cassio".

77. Cassio and Caterina Avella

2343

Form 2202.—I.
U. S. DEPARTMENT OF LABOR
NATURALIZATION SERVICE

TRIPLICATE

No. _____

CA 139967

93332

UNITED STATES OF AMERICA
DECLARATION OF INTENTION
☞ Invalid for all purposes seven years after the date hereof

State of New York, ⎫
County of Bronx, ⎬ ss:
⎭   In the Supreme Court of Bronx County.

I, _____ Domenico Nicassio _____, aged __30__ years,
occupation __Actor__, do declare on oath that my personal
description is: Color white, complexion __Dark__, height __5feet __6__ inches,
weight __138__ pounds, color of hair __Black__, color of eyes __Brown__
other visible distinctive marks __None__
I was born in __Canneto, Italy__
on the __28th__ day of __November__, anno Domini 1 __897__; I now reside
at __455 E. 138th St.__, New York City, N. Y.
                    (Give number and street)
I emigrated to the United States of America from __Naples, Italy__
on the vessel __Giuseppe Verdi__; my last
        (If the alien arrived otherwise than by vessel, the character of conveyance or name of transportation company should be given)
foreign residence was __Canneto, Italy__; I am __not__ married; the name
of my ⎧wife⎫ is _____, ⎧she⎫ was born at _____
       ⎩husband⎭   ⎩he ⎭
and now resides at _____
It is my bona fide intention to renounce forever all allegiance and fidelity to any foreign
prince, potentate, state, or sovereignty, and particularly to _____
        __Victor Emmanuel III, King of Italy__
of whom I am now a subject; I arrived at the port of __NY__
in the State of __NY__, on or about the __8th__ day
of __September__, anno Domini 1 __922__; I am not an anarchist; I am not a
polygamist nor a believer in the practice of polygamy; and it is my intention in good faith
to become a citizen of the United States of America and to permanently reside therein:
SO HELP ME GOD.

_____
(Original signature of declarant)

Subscribed and sworn to before me in the office of the Clerk of said Court
at New York City, N. Y., this __25__ day of __Apr 11__
[SEAL]   anno Domini 192__8.__

Robert L. Moran
SPECIAL DEPUTY
Clerk of the Supreme Court.

14—1887   By _____, Deputy Clerk.

78. Cassio's application for U.S. residency.

207

79. Inscription on reverse of *Who Am I?* cast photograph.

80. Cast of *Who Am I?* photograph (left to right) cameraman, Caterina Avella, Cassio, actress as maid, director John L. McCutcheon, actor as butler and Natacha Rambova.

81. Natacha Rambova & Cassio in *Who Am I?*

Having Their Say...

Howe, Wehner & Mundy

Her Years as Valentino's Wife

Why Natacha Rambova's Marriage to the Greatest of Screen Idols came to a Tragic End

By HERB HOWE
The New Movie Magazine, December 1929-May 1930.

Passing the Vesuvio, an obscure little Italian restaurant in the basement of a brownstone front directly behind the Capitol Theatre in New York, I was stopped by gusts of memory. It was here I often lunched and dined with Rudie Valentino, who with characteristic sentiment remained loyal to the place long after fame offered him its caviar.

Memory-drawn, I turned and went down the few steps to the arched entrance beneath the stairs that led to the floor above. The one window of the place gazed at me lifelessly, shrouded in curtains a little soiled. Faint eddies of dust whirled on the stone pavement in the corner by the door as if they also were seeking entrance. A few folded papers, soggy and stained and dead, lay there. Across the arched opening under the stairs an iron lattice grating had been drawn so that the vestibule to the inner door was dark and hollow like a tomb. The grating was padlocked.

It, too, was gone.

In the still dreariness I recalled our last evening there. I had come alone to dine on the good but cheap table d'hote. There were several diners in the place, mostly Italians and their girls. I took a small table by the kitchen door where I could exchange words with the plump signora who emerged steaming from time to time to look over her guests. I had come to know her through Rudie. He always exchanged banter and Italian compliments with her.

The waiter was in the act of placing my plate of minestrone when a hush fell on the room like a stroke of paralysis. The plate of soup remained suspended beneath my nose as though the waiter had turned to bronze, and the spoons and forks of the other diners were similarly transfixed in mid-air. The whole room was stricken by the opening of the outer door.

"*Buona sera*," called the husky voice of the signora, coming out of the kitchen to greet the arrivals. "*Buona sera, signora, come sta?*" boomed the reply, and then the same voice, "Hello, Herb, come have dinner with us." Rudie had entered, working his usual spell, and with him Natacha, his wife, and Natacha's white-haired aunt, to whom Rudie was so devoted that in his last will he named her affectionately his beneficiary.

I moved to their table and tried to feel at ease among the surrounding waxworks. Rudie never appeared conscious of stares. He enjoyed attention and accepted it with lusty naturalness where other stars are rendered coyly artificial.

The other people in the restaurant recognized the Valentinos, of course, but their eyes—the only mobile parts left them—turned queryingly on me. I spilled my soup with hands that behaved as if in husking mittens. Apparently my identity had to be explained to spare me the inconvenience of developing apoplexy. "If they don't stop staring," I said, my complexion ripening to mauve, "I shall arise and announce I'm the late John Bunny staging a come-back."

Rudie released a hearty guffaw and the diners thawed. The dinner went merrily with Natacha's wit; Rudie had a huge appetite for humor as well as for food.

That was our last dinner ... A vivid memory.

Turning from the bleak little ristorante, barred and sealed, its own mausoleum, I vowed to find Natacha at once and lunch and laugh once more.

NATACHA RAMBOVA. The name in letters of stone appear above a shop next to Fifth Avenue at Fifty-second Street. Rich fabrics and pieces of antique jewelry are in the window, beyond which your curious gaze is lost in folds of gauzy green.

I opened the door. In the center of a spacious salon, modernistically spare, with furnishings of silver and burgundy, stood that dominant, regal girl, dressed in black velvet, her small head turbaned in flame with braids of brown hair coiled close to her ears — the girl who in her own words has been called "everything from Messalina to a dope fiend."

214

I expected to find her restrained. A volume of tragedy has been written since that night we parted over the gay Italian meal. Unmercifully flayed after her separation from Rudie, she went for seclusion to her mother in France. She re-emerged briefly at the time of Rudie's death, then disappeared again. I knew there had been shabby years. People reported seeing her now and then on the Avenue. She was always alone, dressed severely plainly, but her head was held high by that indomitable will of hers. She tried many things; vaudeville, dancing classes, writing, decorating. Finally, a small shop, then success and a larger one. All the friends of her opulent hour passed her by long ago; her clientele has been built solely on her art as designer and is strictly Park Avenue, without a stage or screen celebrity.

Even her worst enemy has admitted the genius of Natacha, that unquenchable flame of ambition that sweeps out from her ruthlessly to combat Hollywood and its intrigues implacable instinct, a fighting' spirit of Amazonian fierceness. Yet, for all her electric vitality, I think Natacha's spirit is a little weary. Very young, she has witnessed with shrewd eyes the mockery of the world's spectacle, and from the highest throne of idolatry this age has known, she has experienced its sharp irony.

I recalled the days I spent in her apartment collaborating with Rudie on his life story. Because of some legal technicality pertaining to his divorce from Jean Acker, he and Natacha were forced to maintain separate apartments for several months after their marriage in Mexico, but of course Rudie spent most of the time in Natacha's.

There was a moment of constraint as Natacha and I set down on the divan. To break it, I referred to the hours spent on his life story. "Now we ought to do your life," I said. "But I guess all your real names have been told." "Yes, and I've been called a lot of names that weren't mine," laughed Natacha. "No, I'm here to tell you right now that I don't give a hang for publicity. God knows there has been too much for me already. I've been called everything from Messalina to a dope-fiend." "Did you feel it much?" "I was tortured. I was tortured to agony," she said. Her eyes met mine in an eloquence of silence. In that minute the interval of years passed by. I felt certain I knew her as I hadn't before.

She turned the poignancy of the revelation with a quick laugh. I always loved the laughter of Natacha. It is clear and gay. And

215

it can shield a multitude of sorrows with its courage. "They even said I have no sense of humor!" Her laugh mounted. "That's equivalent to saying I am dead. Without it, I would have been, long ago."

Those who said it couldn't have known that her real name is O'Shaughnessy. No more did those who thought to defeat her.

In the Hollywood days, the studio rang with her battles for Rudie, his stories, his salary, his costumes. "Oh, I was a fool," she exclaimed with a rueful smile. "But I was young and optimistic and full of fight. I didn't realize the uselessness. I was butting my head against a wall. They don't care about your ideas or about you. They want to crowd as many pictures into as little time as possible, to collect on you as swiftly as they can. What happens to the star is of no concern."

"I can't think of any position more difficult than that of an idol's wife," I said. "It was hellish," she affirmed. "Rudie hadn't one faint gleam of business sense. He knew he hadn't and relied on me. He was a big, sweet, trusting child who wanted to be loved above all things. And that desire to be liked by everyone left him open to imposition. He would agree to anything to be agreeable. When he realized he had made a mistake, I rushed into them shouting, 'No!' And you know how popular that word is in Hollywood!

This of course gave them a fine weapon against me. Everyone knew Rudie was sweet and agreeable at all times, therefore if anyone suffered it was because of *Mrs.* Valentino. A girl would be presented for a part. Perhaps she was five feet eight and the part called for a kitten. I would say I couldn't see her as the type. The girl was dismissed: 'Mrs. Valentino didn't like you.'

"It was fiendish. Yet I felt I was necessary. Rudie felt I was, you know that. But he had pride, a legitimate man's-pride, and they worked on that. They commenced bringing him clippings which said 'Mrs. Valentino wears the pants,' 'too bad Rudie can't be his own boss,' and so forth and so forth. These rankled. Eventually, if I so much as observed it was a nice day, Rudie, about to agree, would catch himself and say, 'No, it is *not!*' Of course I realized how he felt. He didn't want to be putty even in his wife's hands. We would laugh about the clippings; nevertheless, they made a wedge.

Rudie was frightfully sensitive. He couldn't stand the least criticism. And being an actor—a much finer actor than most people realized, he was pliant. If I shaped some of his convictions, I at least had his interest at heart. Others at the studio—the clipping-bearers,

216

for instance—did not. They imposed on him in every way conceivable. They borrowed money, they took his time, they sold his stuff, and one of his closest 'friends,' I discovered, was speculating in the market with his money. A trusting soul, if there ever was one, it was dreadful to open Rudie's eyes to people who appeared so nice to him, who he thought *liked* him.

"I would kill off one crop of sycophants and—so help me!—the next morning there would be another. I never saw anything to equal it. They sprang up overnight like toadstools. Only a person who has experienced Hollywood would believe me. They not only wanted to get in his good graces, each wanted to monopolize him utterly. And when they couldn't they said I did!

"Oh, I tell you it was sweet for me." She laughed a little ruefully. "I can't understand now how I ever could have been so foolish as to let it wear me down. It did. You lose perspective.

It's inevitable that you lose it. They force you out of your mind. Perhaps if you could go through it first and then go back . . . but you have to go through it to know. You simply cannot keep your perspective.

Another thing, I didn't want to go to parties. I'm not a particularly sociable mortal. I didn't care for society and didn't go before, and I couldn't see any reason for going after we were in a certain position. That of course did not endear me with people who wanted the Valentinos for show pieces at their affairs. I didn't care if I was unpopular, but it hurt Rudie to be. Deeply ingrained in him was the desire for popularity, to be liked.

I remember the first day he came on to the set, I disliked him. At that time, I was very serious, running about in low-heeled shoes and taking squints at my sets and costumes. Rudie was forever telling jokes and forgetting the point of them, and I thought him plain dumb," Natacha laughed. "Then it came over me suddenly one day that he was trying to please, to ingratiate himself with his absurd jokes. Of course I capitulated. 'Oh, the poor child,' I thought. 'He just wants to be liked—he's lonely. . . .' And, well, you know what that sentiment leads to. . . ."

Rudie was lonely. I never knew a lonelier man. He craved affection so. I remember the first time he spoke Natacha's name to me. We had had dinner in his one-room-and-kitchenette apartment in the Formosa. He had engaged a woman to come in and serve for the occasion, and it was wistfully festive. I had done the first stories about him, he was deeply grateful. Hollywood, for him, was a forlorn place until his success was firmly decided. They looked upon him as a dubious Italian with sleek hair who had been a tango dancer in a cabaret, who was pathetically poor and altogether of no consequence in film society. Even after New York recognized him as an artist in "The Four Horsemen," Hollywood sat back in its provincial smugness and had to be shown. Rudie showed me some of his first notices proudly. While I was waxing sincerely fervent over his prospects, he tentatively ventured the name of Natacha Rambova. Had I heard of her? I hadn't. She was doing some really remarkable sets, he said. He thought her a fine artist. Perhaps my magazine might be interested in some of her drawings to publish. His suggestion was so timorous I gave no importance to it. On another evening, sometime later, as we sat until the revealing hours of morning over coffee in a downtown cafe, he told me:

"She is a wonderful girl, very much alone like myself. I go to her house evenings and we talk about things that interest us, things that don't seem to interest many people here; books, new plays, the modern art movement, and of course our work. Our tastes are very similar. It is just a friendship, which I need very much. I don't know where it will lead. I hope it will keep on growing."

Then after their marriage: "There was nothing mad or hysterical about our love. It commenced slowly in friendship, as I told you, and just blossomed naturally. She gives me companionship, sincere and sympathetic companionship—the thing I have always longed for, the thing a man needs above all else to complete himself."

Their separation was one of the many great tragedies that may be laid at the gates of Hollywood, most worldly of places on earth today. For the idol it is a garden of many blandishments, the sireny of which, continually repeated, leads to dizziness if not destruction.

I do not believe Natacha ever departed from the mind of Rudie, nor actually from his heart. He was proud, he had been wounded and was confused, yet over his last will when he was ill his thoughts must have hovered over their associations, for he named, with deep affection, her aunt who was a symbol of them. "It was Hollywood that separated you," I said to Natacha. She only nodded.

Do you think it possible for two people to succeed with marriage there?" I asked, "not just ostensibly I mean, but actually? ...

218

or even with great friendship?" "The only possibility, I think," she said, "would be if they kept entirely out of it all and recognized it for what it's worth. But ah! —that's it. You are young, appearances are deceptive; you don't realize you are losing perspective and being absorbed until you are swallowed up."

"Hollywood is a hot-bed of malice. It seethes and boils in envy. Never a good word is spoken of anyone unless for publicity or to gain some personal end. Sweet words of flattery have vinegar on their breath. Eyes of malevolence watch you and even as you turn you feel the tearing tongues of back biters. People go places out of fear. Fear is on parade: fear of being forgotten if you are not in the procession, fear of being talked about if you stay away and fear of the ravening critical eyes when you are present.

"It's a terrible place. Thank God I'm out of it all!" She spoke with mirthful detachment even of Hollywood, with an amused mockery that embraced herself. "It's like the war," I said. "You can laugh at it all when it's over." "Exactly," she said. "And particularly at your own ridiculous self, taking it so seriously." "And you will never return?" "Well, hardly! I haven't heard from anyone there and never expect to hear. ..."

The telephone rang an interruption. "Who is it?" she asked the assistant. "Some studio. ... I don't get the name. ..." Natacha was aghast. . .. "Can you beat that! Speak of the devil and. . . . You brought this on!" She went to the phone. "Believe me or not," said she, returning. "They called to ask me where the 'Beaucaire' costumes are that I designed six years ago. Beat that! How in the world should I know where their costumes are?"

"You'll have to go back, Natacha," I said solemnly. "You'll have to go back and find those costumes for them or they'll add *thief* to your string of names." But Natacha was reduced to muttering astonishment and didn't heed me. "Now what on earth possessed them to call me . . . How did they know where I was . . . My heavens!"

Last year Natacha designed the sets and costumes for the American opera at the Champs Elysees Theater in Paris. They received the marked attention of artists and critics. It was suggested that she should return to the cinema as an art director. "You were ahead of your time before," they said.

"Yes, I'm always ahead of my time and getting kicked out for it," mused Natacha. "Never again!

219

"No sir, I'm content sitting right here," she said, glancing around her shop. "I am a business woman and I shall continue one until. ..." A transient shadow passed over her eyes, a trifle weary, and I knew the vaulting spirit of Natacha had touched futility "until I can go off to live in an adobe shack with some books, at the end of nowhere. ..."

She looked at me now, the amused expression she had maintained through the conversation faded out.

"I am glad Rudie died when he did; while the world still adored him. The death of his popularity would have been a thousand deaths to him. Rudie belonged to the age of romance. He brought it with him; it went with him. I think it was a climax he would have wished. I'm sure of it."

I said, "He died still in that fabulous dream of romance such as few men on earth have had, so the tragedy of awakening was averted. And I believe the last words he would have spoken were those that wrung our hearts in "The Four Horsemen," the words of *Julio* dying in a trench in France: *Je suis content.*

The Valentino Death Prophecy

A world famous medium tells in his own words how he pierced the veil between the living and the dead and predicted the death of the great actor in the presence of his glamorous wife, Natacha Rambova.

Mystic Science Magazine, November 1938.

I, George Wehner, known to the public as the Valentino medium, am one of those whose nervous organisms are vibrational receiving sets. When I am in a state of trance, people who are no longer living in physical bodies come to me and translate their vibrational-waves into terms of concrete thought.

In 1926, while I was engaged to give séances to the family of Mr. and Mrs. Richard Hudnut at their Chateau Juan-les-Pins in the south of France, a most remarkable and now world famous prophecy was transmitted through my instrumentality. The story of this prophecy was reported in headlines in leading newspapers and had been the subject of much writing and debate. But it has never been told from the viewpoint of the medium through whom it was given to the world.

It happened one night in August. The Chateau Juan-les-Pins, on its high, rocky prominence overlooking the Mediterranean loomed up huge and white in the bright moonlight. It was the night on which our weekly séance group met to commune with those who wished to get in touch with us from other planes of life.

After dinner we lingered for a while on the broad chateau terrace. In the party were Mr. and Mrs. Richard Hudnut, Natacha Rambova, their daughter and the recently divorced wife of Rudolph Valentino, her Aunt Teresa and most beloved friend of Rudy, "Aunt Tessy", some friends and I. As we sat and watched the day die out behind the misty mountains of the Esterel, a silence fell upon the little group.

Natacha had received a cable from George Ullman, Valentino's manager, stating that Rudy had become ill in New York and that he was to be operated upon. As we knew that Rudy had always enjoyed splendid health and possessed great vitality, we felt that his illness could not be serious and yet we were all greatly concerned. Natacha, who really loved Rudy sincerely, was especially disturbed.

As is usual before a séance, I began to grow extremely sensitive-to feel the vibratory emanations from my surroundings. I felt the pressing nearness of another world and the penetrating intermingling of the auras of souls passed on. Then one came nearer who brushed repeatedly against the astral antenna of my nerves and prompted me with an almost overwhelming desire to express his eager message.

Beyond the terrace, in a tree at the edge of the bright moonlight, a nightingale began its song of love. It was the hour for us to begin the séance. We all arose and went into the great stone hall of the chateau hung with rare and ancient tapestries and we climbed the winding marble stairs.

The séance was held in a large room with balconied windows overlooking the Mediterranean. We took our accustomed places in the circle and Mrs. Hudnut switched off the lights in the hanging crystal chandelier and threw a veil over the room's sidelights, dimming them to the softness required. There was enough light for us to see each other's forms and faces clearly.

As we sat silently in our chairs in the midst of that luxurious chamber, I felt we were but duplicating a practice of the ancient Druids, those almost forgotten mystics who used to sit in just such a circle against great stones on some English moor. Yes, like them we sat and waited-waited for the voices that would soon speak to us from out the silence. Through the open windows the song of the nightingale poured in, its notes pouring forth in a kind of wild ecstasy.

"Never before have I heard a bird sing like that", remarked Natacha. "I'm going to close the windows. I can't stand it. It makes me think of Hollywood days and Rudy."

It was as though the song of the nightingale marked the love that had been between Natacha and Rudy. Natacha shut the window and returned to her chair. Mrs. Hudnut began to recite the Lord's Prayer and we all joined in. A subtle change now swept over the room. The atmosphere which at our entrance had been static, now suddenly seemed alive and vibrant, charged with aural currents. I began to see the dim, shadowy forms of ghostly people crowding through the ether towards us.

As I looked about the circle I could not help comparing the two kinds of living personalities in the room, the living alive and the living dead! Richard Hudnut, at seventy, serenely charming and debonair, Mrs. Hudnut with her red-gold hair and eyes of pale jade, Natacha Rambova, calm and stately in emerald satin and gold lamé, her finely chiseled features and dark eyes set off by a turban of vermillion - and then, these astral visitors so dim to our perceptions, yet more real and tangibly enduring than any of us on earth.

A drowsiness, as of a murmur of low-voiced music, began now to steal across my senses, a preliminary sign of approaching trance. How willingly the psychic yields to this delirious drowsiness that sets free the spirit!

The state of trance has been described by many scientists, but I believe the best definition is that given and signed by Dr. George Hyslop and acceded to by such eminent authorities as Morton Prince, Alfred Moll, Pierre Janet and William McDougall.

"Trance," said Dr. Hyslop, "is a form of mental disassociation. It is an alteration in consciousness characterized by restriction of mental activities with a proportionate failure to react to environmental stimuli in the ordinary manner. Trance may vary in form as well as degree of depth."

As I let myself fall swiftly into this state, the sounds in the room became rapidly magnified. The creaking of chairs sounded like the scrunching of forest branches and the breathing of the sitters resembled the roaring of the winds. The nightingale outside seemed scarcely dimmed by the walls and his rich melody now filled my heart with a feeling of impending doom. Finally, all these sounds mingled together into one confused, chaotic jumble and became a roar so deafening that I could stand it no longer. I became unconscious.

What now occurred I repeat from the records made by those present who witnessed the phenomena. Those who study the occult seriously, as did the members of our circle, make careful note of all manifestations. Each movement of the medium, each word uttered, becomes significant and is recorded. I only hear what has happened when I emerge from the trance.

I sank against the high back of my chair, my head tipped slightly to one side. For a few moments my breathing became heavy and labored, then it grew slower and finally seemed to cease almost entirely. The mouth fell open and the muscles of the face twitched slightly.

Now a startling change took place. All relaxation disappeared, my body straightened itself and I sat bolt upright and became intensely animated as though by a strong electric presence. My lips drew together and suddenly a whistle, low, melodious and clear streamed forth into the room. The sound increased to a remarkably full round tone which rose and fell in a burst of wild melody. This phenomenon of whistling was well known to the sitters and invariably started a séance.

It was always done through one of my two guides, either Frank, a young man who had played the flute in his earth-life or by Zarbo, a gypsy, whose power of improvisation had been tested often by interested musicians.

Then, quite unexpectedly the whistling reached a crescendo and ceased as abruptly as it began. A rustle now swept through the expectant circle for the moment had arrived for the messages to begin.

Voices began to pour from my throat, at first in whispers and incoherent mutterings, then more clearly. The strong voices of men, the softer accents of women, the high treble of children; crying, laughter and conversation all made themselves heard. The still living people spoke whom the world calls dead.

Many of these people, fathers, mothers, sisters and brothers and even the forebears of earlier periods were full and accurately described by Frank and Zarbo, my guides. The facial expressions of these people transfigured my countenance and gestures in familiar mannerisms animated my arms and hands. Not only relatives made themselves known, but friends and friends of friends who came to send messages to people who were not even present at the séance.

The circle became animated. The sitters leaned forward in their eager desire to communicate. Rapid and significant talk passed back and forth between the people of two worlds as they met there in that room. To an outsider, experiencing a first séance, the happenings of this night would have seemed astonishing, if not incredible. But to this group long familiar with such procedure, they were but the usual results.

Suddenly Natacha shuddered, "I felt an icy wind blow through the room," she said, "Did anyone else notice it?"

"I feel it now," exclaimed Mrs. Hudnut.

"And I - and I -," whispered several of the others.

A chill fell upon the group. The lively communications ceased. I slumped back in my chair.

"The room is growing darker," said Mr. Hudnut.

"And yet no one touched the lights," remarked Aunt Tessy.

Sheaths of dark shadows seemed to press in from all sides of the room as if to envelop the circle in veils of blackness. As the atmosphere grew tense, my body came alive and my lips began to move in short, ejaculated speech. My right hand stretched forth eagerly towards Natacha. The voice that now spoke through me was that of a man. It had an Italian accent.

"Natacha! Natacha!" it cried, "I knew you would come!" Natacha looked startled. The voice had the sound of one who was speaking aloud in a troubled dream.

"You knew I would come where?" she asked.

"I love you-I knew you would come back," the voice continued.

"But I don't understand. Come where?"

"New York."

"But, my dear friend," broke in Mrs. Hudnut, "don't be foolish. This is not Manhattan. We are three thousand miles from there -in the south of France."

"New York," persisted the voice drowsily, "New York-New York."

"I have never heard of such a thing," exclaimed Mrs. Hudnut with a touch of annoyance, "One would think-"

"Hush, Mother," quieted Natacha, "This is something unusual. Let him speak to me."

"Natacha, where are you? Where are you? Don't go away," pleaded the voice.

"Yes, I am Natacha all right and I won't go away. But tell me please, who you are."

The circle rustled with expectation.

"Who are you?"

"Rudy," replied the voice, betraying now a vague, quivering excitement." I knew you would come. I knew you would come."

Natacha did not answer. She sat still and silent. In that shadowy room her suddenly pallid face made one think of a pale, white rose.

"Rudy!" exclaimed Aunt Tessy. "I don't believe it. If anything had happened, we would have been notified."

"Certainly," agreed Mrs, Hudnut, "What do you make of it, Natacha?"

But Natacha made no answer. She sat leaning forward, staring at my trembling body with wide, startled eyes.

"Don't you think we ought to break the circle and bring the medium out of the trance?" asked Mrs. Hudnut nervously.

"No, no mother-wait!" Natacha answered. "Something very strange is going on here. That voice sounds almost exactly like Rudy's-and-"

My body continued to move about agitatedly. The voice muttered on, brokenly.

"Natacha-cara mia." The rest of the words came in broken phrases of soft, melodious Italian. It was the more startling, since at the time I knew no Italian.

Natacha replied in the same language.

"What is he saying?" asked Aunt Tessy, her voice betraying a growing anxiety.

"Why," said Natacha, "he seems to think we are in New York and that I have come back to him. I can't understand it. It sounds like Rudy, all right, but just as if he were talking in his sleep."

"If that is Rudy, he would certainly know who I am," said Mrs. Hudnut. "Rudy, dear, speak-do you know who this is?"

But the presence in my body paid no heed to Mrs. Hudnut's request. I sat upright again and my closed eyes opened and stared upward. Then a cry came from my throat.

"Jenny!"

"What does he mean by Jenny?" demanded Mrs. Hudnut.

"Why, Jenny," said Natacha, "was the mother of June Mathis, who wrote the scenario of 'The Four Horsemen'. Rudy used to live in Jenny's home and she was very helpful to him when he first went to Hollywood."

Now the voice spoke again, saying the name, "Gabriella-Gabriella."

"That is the name of Rudy's mother," cried Natacha. "Are you Rudy's mother?"

"Si-Gabriella."

She then expressed her concern for her son. Rudy had not yet died, she explained. "He is lying ill in New York. But he will not

226

recover. In a very few days he will pass out of his body as you call it. He will die. His time on earth is done. I have come to be near him at the moment of death. I am glad that I passed on first, for now I can help him in the hour of need. As I gave him to the earth in birth, so now in re-birth I can give him to the life eternal. He will go on Monday."

"Why, that will be August the 23rd. That's next Monday."

"Yes, on that day he will come to me," answered Gabriella.

The circle now became so excited that the current of communication was broken and I came out of the trance state and regained consciousness. Everyone was talking excitedly. No one believed it had been Rudy speaking-except Natacha. The others thought that some mischievous entity had spoken in order to create a sensation by pretending to be Rudy. I was disturbed over this, too, but I felt so gloomy and depressed that I thought there must be more to this than the circle was willing to admit.

In a few days Natacha received another cable from Mr. Ullman giving us the cheerful news that Rudy's operation had been successful and that soon the patient could leave the hospital well on the road to recovery. We were all cheered up and delighted. Natacha cabled daily to Rudy and he to her and a reconciliation took place between them.

We talked of nothing else. It seemed now that the séance had been entirely wrong and we were sure that Rudy's apparent coming had been only an impersonation by another.

But Natacha and I were still bewildered-the voice had sounded so like Rudy's. Then there was the fact of the Italian language-the appearance of his mother, Gabriella and the "Jenny" episode. It was all a little too strange.

We talked of Rudy's life. Of his childhood in Italy and his struggles in America. Natacha told of how she had first met him in a Hollywood studio through Alla Nazimova, the great Russian actress, for whom she was art director at that time. She spoke of the beginning of his fame-the triumph of "The Four Horsemen". And she spoke of Rudy's psychic powers.

Few people knew that Valentino was a medium and had developed the power to do automatic writing. Natacha told us fascinating stories of how Rudy used to give impromptu séances at the home of Jenny and of June Mathis.

And now it seemed, from the Ullman cable that Rudy would

227

continue his life on earth unbroken and that he would remain the romantic, passionate lover of the screen-the idol of the entire world.

That night we held another séance. Almost at once, two of Rudy's spirit guides, who used to write through him, manifested through me-Black Feather, an American Indian and Mesolope, an Egyptian.

Mesolope told the eager group, in as gentle a manner as possible that the time of Rudy's stay on earth was up; that in spite of the reassuring news we had received from America, Rudy would pass from him body on Monday, August the 23rd. Jenny now came again and verified this statement.

"I have been with Rudy since his illness," she said," I will be with him when the earthly end comes-and how joyfully will I meet him when he begins his life anew! You remember in the other séance that he called out my name-Jenny. Well, I want you to remember what I am saying. It was at the time they were taking him to the hospital in the ambulance. I was in the ambulance by his side. He opened his eyes, and for a moment he recognized my presence and cried out my name. Just as he did through the medium. Yes, his time is up, his work finished and he will be with us in spirit on Monday next, August 23rd."

Twice the prophecy of death for August 23rd!

The séance ended. The circle broke up. Natacha, Aunt Tessy and Mrs. Hudnut were in tears; the rest of us stricken by the foreboding.

Mr. Hudnut tried to reassure us. "Rudy is so young and strong," he comforted, "the spirits may be wrong. His interest in life may pull him through."

I looked at Natacha standing there, pale in tears and so beautiful. My heart sank. Rudy's interest in life-there it stood, concentrated in the being of that attractive woman. What had he to live for now that she was gone; what comfort was left in the emptiness of fame and wealth when love had fled? No, I thought, Rudy will not *will* to live.

Natacha, as if divining my thoughts turned to her mother and put her arms around her.

"I am frightened," she whispered.

From Paris, Berlin and Vienna the press now invaded the chateau, seeking interviews with the ex-wife of Rudolph Valentino. Natacha would not see them. Mr. Hudnut, who did not realize that we wished no publicity, interviewed the reporters and told them of the two séances. To our astonishment, the following day newspapers all over the world blazed with headlines which told of the prophecy of Valentino's death. Particularly full accounts appeared in the European papers, describing in detail the messages we had received.

On the fatal Monday morning of August 23rd, Natacha came to me and said," This morning when I awoke my room was filled with the odor of the tuberoses. That's a symbol of death, isn't it?"

"Yes," I assented regretfully.

On Tuesday came the delayed cables confirming the death on Monday, August 23rd, of the darling of millions-the departure from earth of Rudolph Valentino. The prophecy had been fulfilled.

We were overwhelmed and stunned by the verity of these séance prophecies. Natacha became ill and was confined to her bed for several days.

Letters arrived from America telling us the details of Rudy's passing. One concerned the séance episode of Rudy's having called out the name of Jenny during my trance. Mr. Ullman stated that while he rode in the ambulance with Valentino, Rudy suddenly looked up and stared at something Ullman could not see-a smile of recognition passed across his face and he had gasped out the very same name-"Jenny!"

This news so impressed Mr. Hudnut that he went to the trouble of finding out the hour when this happened in New York and calculating the five hours' difference, he discovered that in my trance, three thousand miles away, Rudy was calling the name "Jenny!" at the same time. Rudy's brain in the ambulance in New York and my brain in France were for that moment en rapport-operating as one, regardless of time and space or matter. And this communication was received from one who had not yet died!

It was Rudy's great love for Natacha, the one and only real love of his life, that had made this connection possible. Though Rudy was ill, delirious, his one unconscious thought was to reach her whom he loved. I, a psychic, being with his beloved at the time, made the reception of his desire possible.

An Introduction to
A Curious Life by George Wehner

By
Talbot Mundy

To those who are familiar with Spiritualism in its higher and less sensational aspects, Mr. George Wehner needs no introduction. To them he is known as a gentleman sans peur et sans raproche, whose acquaintances respect him and whose friends love him. He is in need of no apologies and no advertisement.

But there are probably hundreds of thousands of people who have never heard of Mr. Wehner, and whose opinions about psychics, clairvoyants, clairaudients and mediums in general were formed from sensational reports in newspapers or in conversation with other people who were equally ignorant and prejudiced. Amazing though the fact may seem to anyone who knows even only a few of the simplest proven facts about Spiritualism, there are still innumerable people who believe, because they have been told so by somebody else, that nothing ever takes place at a mediumistic séance which cannot be explained away as either trickery or hallucination.

Many other people have been prejudiced by the mistakes of undeveloped, and now and then of dishonest mediums, whose unwise methods and unsatisfactory phenomena have aroused suspicions. And there are hundreds of thousands who yearn for definite assurance of life after death and for intelligible facts with which to re-enforce and confirm their faith in religious teaching, but who are forbidden by the rules of their denomination or the prejudices of their families and friends from investigating themselves. As an incurable rebel against ungrounded prejudice and unproven authority, I recommend this book as an antidote against that sickness of the human mind; that paralysis of common sense which seizes on the best of us at times and on some of us all the time, preventing us from accepting or even studying facts which the majority is afraid to recognize, or which the temporary, usually self-elected leaders of opinion tell us are "beneath contempt."

Truth is, and always has been beneath contempt-beneath it and above it. Contempt may be likened to the sand into which the fabled ostrich sticks its head. It is the emotion exhibited by bigots and it is the substance of the smoke-cloud they emit when they propose to protect their bigotry at all costs, but preferably in the easiest way. Contempt resembles the effluvium exuded by the common and more admirable (because less dishonest) skunk.

Its ultimate form is self-contempt, which is fortunately self-destructive. It was contempt which led the recognized authorities of that day to imprison Galileo for declaring that the world moves. It attacked even Newton, who was possibly too busy with the truth to pay attention to it. It persecuted the alchemists, who were the fathers of modern chemistry. We have all seen it leveled at Einstein, Sir Oliver Lodge and Sir Arthur Conan Doyle. Jesus, we are told on good authority, was despised by the pundits of His day; and it is a matter of common record that every teacher who has genuinely tried to get at the truth of what Jesus taught, and the mother-lode of truth behind his teaching, has been scurrilously persecuted by that bitterly alert lower instinct of those who think they have something to lose if the truth were revealed.

The human mind is an incorrigible coward. It craves company in its cowardice and it hates (as it hated Jesus) all those individuals who dare to prove that the realms of thought are infinitely larger and more free to roam in that conventional opinion says they are. It dreads the Infinite. It fears unknown dimensions. And above all it detests responsibility. Hysterically it hates the thought that individual responsibility for every word and deed is inescapable and sooner or later must be faced. It seeks to hide from such elementary justice behind whatever cloak convention offers. Ridicule, calumny, clamor-anything will serve-"Great is our Diana of the Ephesians!" And it picks up any stone available to fling at whoever challenges the manhood and love of truth which we hope-which we would like to think-which we pretend, at any rate, to think resides somewhere in every one of us.

Of course, the easiest stone to fling at Spiritualists is the accusation of self-deception and chicanery. Sir Oliver Lodge, for instance, who admittedly understands more scientific laws and knows more of nature's method than most of his critics ever dream of, is "self-deceived." Being equipped with a splendid brain, enriched and disciplined by fifty years of scientific and sustained inquiry into the laws that govern natural forces and their phenomena, he, who has studied Spiritualism, is an obvious target for the contempt of those who have not studied it. He, who can measure atoms and the velocity of light and who talks with his son who was slain in the war, obviously is a proper object for the ridicule of critics who can do none of these things and who probably lack the ambition to do them. It is always easier to ridicule a thinker than to think.

It would be interesting to meet an opponent of Spiritualism who had actually devoted to its critical study one ten-thousandth of the patient zeal that daily is devoted to invention of new tooth-paste or the concoction of boot-leg liquor.

It should be borne in mind that to be worth attention, criticism must be fair. Prejudice is probably not separable from the human mind at this stage of its evolution, but fairness is possible, even if difficult. At least nine-tenths of the allegedly scientific "tests" of psychic phenomena made by the opponents of Spiritualism have been made under conditions so grossly unfair as to make their production and proof problematic, if not impossible.

For instance: if we could challenge a great artist to paint a picture under our hostile gaze, clothed in uncomfortable garments of our choosing, in a place of our selection, in an atmosphere of suspicion, would it be logical or just to brand him a "faker" if he should generously accept the challenge but produce a mere "daub"? Or place a poet in the same predicament-or a composer of music. Or subject to a similar test a group of bankers, with a difficult problem in high finance to be worked out in a room crowded with suspicious enemies alert to challenge every spark of genius before it could enlarge itself into a flame. Would any responsible group of bankers accept such a challenge? Or would a surgeon agree to perform a major operation under such conditions?

Whoever has done inspirational work of any kind knows what it means to wear an old coat or to sit in a familiar chair in a friendly environment. We may not know why these are an aid to inspiration and those who merely criticize our work instead of doing their own may call us fools for our attachment to the coat or the chair; nevertheless, we know-and they are merely advertising what they do not know.

In the same way, a medium knows exactly under which conditions he can best become a channel for the forces that it is proposed shall use him; and he has as much right to specify those conditions as an electrician or a photographer, or a poet or a musician has to specify the conditions under which he will produce what is demanded of him. Who would challenge a photographer to take a portrait in a dim room filled with red smoke? Obviously, no one but an imbecile.

And none but an ignoramus or a dishonest photographer with a trick up his sleeve, or an unwise optimist who hoped to take advantage of some fluke of light and smoke, would consent to such a test. Yet, mediums are frequently challenged to meet more trying tests than any of those mentioned; and they are denounced if they refuse to try to produce their delicate phenomena while surrounded by thought forms and vibrations that make the task impossible. The marvel is that they succeed as often as they do, nor that they fail now and then.

The charge of fraud is frequent and is sometimes proven. It would be miraculous if that were not so; it would, in fact, be more miraculous than any of the miracles of religion or science. No reasonable person would pretend to expect to find exclusively saintly adventurers into such an unexplored field as Spiritualism admittedly is. The time to make wholesale imputations of fraud against mediums as a class may suitably, perhaps, begin when in the prisons of the world there are no judges, ministers of the Gospel, reformers, scientists, doctors, bankers, editorial writers, reporters-it may be fair, perhaps, when even one social layer or profession is no longer represented in the amazing lists of criminals that are a matter of public record.

Mediums are human. They include among their number many ignorant as well as many highly educated people. The very sensitiveness of their organism makes it difficult for some of them to earn a living at the ordinary, humdrum tasks. Nevertheless, they need money. That same sensitiveness has made many an undeveloped medium temporarily incapable of functioning; inexperience, and possibly personal vanity has combined with the need of money to induce him, nevertheless to make the attempt; and natural human obliquity has sometimes tempted some of them to resort to trickery to offset ill-health or whatever the determining cause of incapacity may be.

Some inexperienced mediums-perhaps carried away by the spirit of showmanship, or fun-possibly, like Barnum, eager to provide sensation-or, in other instances, actuated by a characteristically human wish to score off their opponents have countered unfair critical methods with equally reprehensible deception. Undoubtedly some criminals are mediums, just as some are politicians, artists, religious fanatics and so on. Do we prohibit the medical use of morphia because some rascals use it wrongly?

By no means are all mediums as highly developed or of as unquestionably high personal character as Mr. George Wehner, although there are others of like quality and equal integrity. It is unfortunate, though true, that there are "quacks", crooks and incompetents in the ranks of Spiritualism as in very other walk of life.

The attempt has been frequently made to indict and condemn every professional medium for the lapses of some from high standards of ethics; but does the attempt convince the logical observer of anything except the malignity, or stupidity or both, of the accusers making that attempt? Do we condemn religion and all religionists because of the behavior of certain priests? Do we condemn literature because of certain journalists? Is law repudiated because legislators have been hanged?

Doctors have made mistakes of diagnosis, causing the death or failing to prevent the death of so many victims that it would be impossible to make a list of them; ignorant doctors have probably killed more people than all wars and all the hangmen every did-but shall we therefore stop investigation of the laws that govern health and sickness and entirely ignore the fact that most doctors are honorable men and many of them have performed what amounts to miracles of healing?

Dame Partington with her broom, trying to sweep back the broad Atlantic, was no more futile than the fanatics are who seek to stay, with their "contempt", this latter-day tide of awakening that seems (I make no claim to more than surmise based on study) to

234

have started simultaneously with the assault by Helena Petrovna Blavatsky ("H.P.B.") on the case-hardened shell of organized and willful ignorance-so profitable for the few and so cruelly hard on the many. It is since her heroic challenge to *the powers that thought they were* that common consciousness has loosed itself and all the sciences have so invaded the Unknown that no man any longer dares to limit them or say where knowledge must eventually cease. Are the shackles that bind religion bursting day by day?

It seems so, although some of the shackled seem to hope not. Do the stars grow nearer, and more familiar, though the lenses of such telescopes as man's imagination hardly dared to hint at fifty years ago? Newspapers herald the fact. In the subway I have heard stenographers discussing Spiral Nebulae, with utterly astonishing inaccuracy. It is true and with a sense of limitation like a mouse's in a trap. But it seems to me that is better than to swear the Spiral Nebulae do not exist and to accuse as charlatans and liars those who say they see them through their telescopes.

Those Spiral Nebulae are distant; millions of light years distant. Birth and death are so much nearer to us that comparison makes loom that door of death through which we all go presently-to what? Is speculation idle or immoral? Is it vain or lacking in common sense and dignity to wish to glimpse beyond that veil; with the purpose, possibly, in mind of using this life as better preparation for the next one that it might be if we slumbered this one in careless ignorance? Who was it told us to awake?

I, of my own knowledge, know that Mr. Wehner is a medium through whom, at times, such wisdom speaks as is not to be found in books. In circumstances under which no fraud was possible, while he was in complete trance, in an apartment in which he had never previously been, such information came through him as could not possibly have been obtained by human agency, or by thought reading or thought transference in any ordinary meaning of those terms.

No more than Mr. Wehner am I interested in convincing any person who prefers to continue in ignorance; nor do I wish to introduce him to those specialists whose *modus vivendi* is based on money received for slanderous assaults on the integrity of others.

But I do suggest that jealousy (a not incurable complaint) has blinded some folk to the truth that certain others can, and do communicate with the deathless spirits of the so-called dead, to the mutual advantage of both "dead" and "living".

And to those not prejudiced by fear, conceit, superstition or jealousy beyond the point where they can recognize integrity of statement and of purpose, it is my sincere pleasure to recommend Mr. George Wehner's book as an entertaining and illuminating flashlight on a scientific problem, that which I believe there is none more challenging, important and inspiring in the world today.

Talbot Mundy

The Appendices

Picture Credits

The sources of photographic material are cited as plate numbers as follows:

Private collection of the author. #4, 6, 7, 14, 17, 18, 19, 21, 22, 23, 36, 43, 49, 51, 75, 76, 78.

The Michael Morris *Madam Valentino* Archive. #1, 5, 20, 34, 38, 39, 40, 41, 42, 50, 52, 64, 68, 69, 73.

The Private Collection of Robert L. Harned. # 8, 9, 54, 55.

The Private Collection of Giovanni Monteleone. #77, 79, 80, 81.

The Roerich Society. #60, 62, 63, 66, 67.

#2-3. Theosophical Society of America Archives.

#15- 16. Film Daily Yearbook, 1926.

#24. Gallica. National Library of France, Digital Library. Bibliotèque Nationale de France. @gallica.bnf.fr

#25. Film Daily Yearbook, 1926.

#28. Province-Alpes-Cote D'Azur, France: Chateau de Juan les Pins (Castle of Crouton) in Antibes on the French Riviera, photo by Dominique Boutin/TASS.

#29. The Casino & Promendade at Juan les Pins, early 1930's - acatamongthepigeons.blogspot.com "Juan les Pins fashion".

#30. The harbor at Juan les Pins - Photo credit © Túrelio (via Wikimedia-Commons), 2006 / Lizenz: Creative Commons CC-BY-SA-2.5

#35. Paul Ivanovitch - By Milan Jovanović (1863–1944) - Blic, Public

Domain, https://commons.wikimedia.org/w/index.php?
curid=14702867

#37. liveauction.com.

#44. Bent, Silas. *Ballyhoo.* New York: Boni and Liveright, 1927.

#45. Mallen, Frank. *Sauce For the Gander.* White Plains, New York:
Baldwin Books, 1954.

#46. Bent, Silas. *Ballyhoo.*

#46a. Mallen, Frank. *Sauce For the Gander.*

#61. Письма Елены Рерих. Т.7" - М.: Международный Центр
Рерихов, 2007, Public Domain.

#70. Maria Salomé, Private Collection. Referenced in *Beyond Valentino
- The Madam Valentino Addendum.*

#71. *Fate Magazine,* March 1956, "Valentino...and His Unseen Guides",
by Robert Gladwell.

#72. *True Mystic Science Magazine.* November 1938.

#74. Natacha Rambova Archive, Yale University, Gift of Edward L
Ochsenschlager in memory of Donald P. Hansen.

Images in Public Domain:

10, 11, 12, 13, 26, 27, 31, 32, 33, 47, 48, 53, 56, 57, 58, 59, 65.

Bibliography

Note: This bibliography reflects research materials and archives referenced in addition to those cited in *Affairs Valentino* and *Beyond Valentino - The Madam Valentino Addendum* bibliographies.

Books:

Andreyev, Alexandre. *The Myth of the Masters Revived, The Occult Lives of Nikolai and Elena Roerich.* Koninklijke Brill, Leiden & Boston: Netherlands, 2014.

Bent, Silas. *Ballyhoo.* New York: Boni and Liveright, 1927.

Bothmer, Bernard V., *Egypt 1950, My First Visit.* Edited by Emma Swan Hall. Oxbow Books, 2003.

Drayer, Ruth A., *Nicholas and Helena Roerich: The Spiritual Journey of Two Great Artists.* Quest Books, Revised Edition, 2005.

Fuller, Loie. *Fifteen Years of a Dancer's Life with Some Account of Her Distinguished Friends.* New York: Restoration Editors, 2015. Originally published in 1913 by Herbert Jenkins Limited. Arundel Place, Haymarket, London S.W., with an introduction by Anatole France.

Harned, Robert L. *Sally Phipps, Silent Film Star.* Published by Robert L. Harned. Brooklyn, New York. June 2015.

Mallen, Frank. *Sauce For the Gander.* White Plains, New York: Baldwin Books, 1954.

Manassa, Colleen and Tasha Dobbin-Bennett. *The Natacha Rambova Archive, Yale University.* Gottinger Miszellen, 234., 2012.

McQuire, William. *Bollingen, An Adventure in Collecting the Past.* Princeton University Press, 1982.

Miccoli, Aurelio. *The Infancy of the Myth.* Translated into English by Angelo Perrone. Turin: Viale Industria Pubblicazioni, 2014.

Morris, Michael. *Madam Valentino, The Many Lives of Natacha*

Rambova. Abbeville Press, 1991.

Morris, Michael and Evelyn Zumaya. *Beyond Valentino - The Madam Valentino Addendum.* Turin: Viale Industria Pubblicazioni, 2017.

Pelley, William Dudley. *Why I Believe The Dead Are Alive!* Noblesville, Indiana: Fellowship Press, 1972.

Schulman, Irving. *Valentino.* New York: Trident Press, a division of Simon & Schuster, Inc., 1967.

Rambova, Natacha. *Rudy - An Intimate Portrait of Rudolph Valentino by His Wife Natacha Rambova.* Paternoster Row, London, E.C.: Hutchinson & Co. December, 1926.

Rambova, Natacha. *Rudolph Valentino: A Wife's Memories of an Icon.* 1921 PVG Publishing, 2009.

Taves, Brian. *Talbot Mundy, Philosopher of Adventure, A Critical Biography.* Jefferson, North Carolina and London: McFarland & Company, Inc., 2006.

Ullman, George. *The S. George Ullman Memoir, The Real Rudolph Valentino by the Man Who Knew Him Best.* Foreword by Evelyn Zumaya. Turin: Viale Industria Pubblicazioni, 2014.

Wehner, George, and Talbot Mundy. *A Curious Life.* New York: Horace Liveright, 1929.

Zumaya, Evelyn. *Affairs Valentino.* Turin: Viale Industria Pubblicazioni, 2015.

Periodicals, News & Magazine Articles:

American Weekly, May 22, 1949. "Genevieve's Daughter".

Beckman, Scott. "William Dudley Pelley: A Life in Right-Wing Extremism and the Occult." *Syracuse University Press,* 2005.

Broenniman, Eleanor Ray. "Mystic India Through Art, *Index to the Messenger, 1913-1927. Vassar, 1899.*

"Business School Review Elects - New Editorial Board Choose Officers for Magazine for 1923-1924". Citation for Edgar Broenniman. *The Harvard Crimson*, October 1, 1923.

Exhibitor's Herald Morning Picture World, July-September 1928.

Exhibitor's Review and Motion Pictures Today, Friday, February 28, 1930.

Exhibitor's Trade Review, August 1925.

Fate Magazine, March 1956, "Valentino...and His Unseen Guides", by Robert Gladwell.

Hulse, Ed. (2009) *The Blood n' Thunder Guide to Collecting Pulps*, Murania Press.

Johnson, Will. "Claude Falls Wright". Accessed on September 9, 2018. https://sites.google.com/site/theosophyhistory/claude-falls-wright.

La Rampe, Paris, 1915-1937.

Life, November 14, 1938.

Stepno, Bob. "The Evening Graphic's Tabloid Reality". www.stepno.com/unc/graphic/

"The Theosophical World View". Theosophical Society of Canada. Accessed on September 9, 2018. https://www.theosophical.ca/about-us1.

True Mystic Science Magazine. November 1938 issue, son of Leslie Grant Scott and R.T.M. Scott, R.T.M. Scott Junior was the magazine's editor in November of 1938.

Archives:

Picture Play Magazine

Motion Picture Magazine

The Chicago Tribune

The Los Angeles Times

The New York Daily News

The New York Times

NARA. National Archive of Registered Aliens,

Cineteca Di Bologna Archive. Bolgna, Italy

Lantern Archives

Gallica, National Library of France, Digital Library. Bibliotèque Nationale de France. @gallica.bnf.fr

New York Public Library archival material @ George Wehner Scores, 1936-1966.

The New York Times archives/1970. "George Wehner Obituary, Special to the New York Times". January 16, 1970.

The New York Public Library, Archives and Manuscripts Division, Alex Rotov Scrapbook, 1939-1948.

World Cat, OCLC, George Wehner Scores, 1936-1966.

The New York Public Library, Register of the Loie Fuller Papers, 1892-1913.

Alex Rotov Scrapbook, The New York Public Library Archives and Manuscripts, The Billy Rose Theater Division.

Simon Fraser University, Library SFU Digital Collections, *Scott, Leslie Grant.* Also information on Leslie Grant Scott cited from: *Woman's Whos Who in America*, (1914-15), Anthony, *History of Women Suffrage Vol. III* (1886), Clippings on Illinois Women Suffrage Association (Fernando Jones Scrapbook) 1875, *Encyclopedia of Chicago*, Chicago Historical Society (Web, 2005), 1900 United States Federal Census, 1930 United States Federal Census.

Find a Grave Memorial. George Benjamin Wehner.

Filmography of Natacha Rambova

1917	*The Woman God Forgot* (costumes)
1920	*Billions* (costumes & sets)
1921	*Forbidden Fruit* (costumes and sets with M. Leisen)
1921	*Aphrodite* (costumes & sets)
1921	*Camille* (costumes & sets)
1922	*A Doll's House* (costume & sets)
1922	*Beyond the Rocks* (costumes)
1922	*The Young Rajah* (costumes & sets)
1923	*Salomé* (costumes & sets)
1924	*Monsieur Beaucaire* (costumes, sets with G. Barbier)
1924	*The Hooded Falcon* (screenplay & costumes, Adrian)
1924	*The Sainted Devil* (costumes with Adrian)
1925	*Cobra* (costumes with Adrian)
1925	*What Price Beauty* (producer & design consultant)
1926	*When Love Grows Cold* (actress)
1928	*Who Am I?* (actress)
1929	*A Light From Saint Agnes*, opera (sets & costumes)

Note: Neither *Aphrodite* or *The Hooded Falcon* were realized as films. *Billions, A Doll's House, The Sainted Devil* and *What Price Beauty* are lost films. Fragments of footage exist of *The Young Rajah* and *When Love Grows Cold*.

Acknowledgements

I wish to thank everyone who contributed to this book by sharing so generously with their time, materials and moral support. This book was immeasurably enhanced through the hard work of the London archivist who wishes to remain anonymous. Their investigative abilities in searching through archives contributed articles, images and new discoveries in Rambova's history; most notably the story of Cassio.

I extend a special thank-you to Robert L. Harned, the author of *Sally Phipps, Silent Film Star*, for his generous, scholarly and enthusiastic contributions to the stories of George Wehner and Alex Rotov. In 1941, Bob Harned's mother, silent film actress, Sally Phipps phoned her friend, celebrity psychic George Wehner on her return to New York City from a trip to India. A gentleman answered the phone in Wehner's apartment that day, informing Ms. Phipps that Mr. Wehner was out. He, Alfred Harned, composer, copyist and instrumentalist, was then transcribing the score for George Wehner's first piano concerto. Sally and Alfred fell in love and married. Their son Robert shared his archives and family stories about his parent's mutual friend, George Wehner which has so enriched the telling of this story.

I would like to thank film historian Dr. Robert J. Kiss for sharing his research on Domenico Nicassio; the transcript of his lecture and images. And a thank-you to Rachel Del Gaudio at the Library of Congress for putting me in touch with Dr. Kiss.

I wish to thank Professor Aurelio Miccoli of Castellaneta, Italy for his expert and successful research in the local archives in the Region of Puglia in search of information about Domenico Niccasio and for his editing of the final drafts of "Cousin Cassio".

I also thank Mr. Giovanni Monteleone for not only sharing the history of his relative Cassio but for granting permission to include his exceptional collection of photographs in this book.

I extend my gratitude to Lucero Rabaudi for this book's cover design. He has created all of the covers for the Viale Industria Pubblicazioni books and his graphic artistry is apparent in each edition.

For Further Reading:

The Viale Industria Pubblicazioni Rudolph Valentino & Natacha Rambova Library:

In English:

Beyond Valentino - The Madam Valentino Addendum

In 1991, Michael Morris published his iconic biography of Natacha Rambova, *Madam Valentino*. He subsequently continued his research, gaining worldwide recognition as the leading Rambova scholar. Those seeking information regarding the disparate aspects of her life and work invariably first contacted Michael Morris. As his Rambova collection grew, he made the decision to open his archive and share ancillary material he did not include in *Madam Valentino*. With the collaboration of co-author, Evelyn Zumaya, the *Madam Valentino Addendum* was realized.

In this, his "final tribute to Rambova", Michael Morris showcases Rambova's written works, her Egyptological scholarship and her study of myth, symbolism and comparative religion. He has included her essay, "Arriba España", excerpts from her unpublished manuscripts and the story of the discovery of a cache of never-before-published photographs and artifacts. Rambova's contemporaries, as well as her intimate circle of associates are profiled, creating an informed and visual glimpse into her later life as well as her esoteric pursuits. This addendum also includes the enlightening contributions of several renowned scholars, who through their respective fields of expertise delve deeper into the life and times of Natacha Rambova.

Affairs Valentino

Evelyn Zumaya's discovery of unpublished court documents and a lost memoir written by Rudolph Valentino's close friend and business manager George Ullman became the basis for her ground-breaking book, *Affairs Valentino*. *Affairs Valentino* challenges the currently held version of the silent film icon's personality,

247

professional life and business affairs. Rich with new anecdotes and never-before-revealed details of Valentino's personal finances and his relationships with family, colleagues, friends and lovers, *Affairs Valentino* is a dramatically different story of Valentino's life than the one that has been repeated for decades. *Affairs Valentino* stands as the ultimate and documented true story of Rudolph Valentino.

The Affairs Valentino Companion Guide

The case file of Rudolph Valentino's probate court records has been missing from its lawful location in the Los Angeles County Hall of Records for decades. With no access to these documents, those endeavoring to tell the tale of the lengthy settlement of the movie star's estate have relied upon surmise and speculation unsupported by facts and figures. As a result, this aspect of Rudolph Valentino's life story has remained a fractionalized, meager and inaccurate account. This would change when Valentino biographer, Evelyn Zumaya conducted a search for the missing archive.

Zumaya discovered that the entire original case file had been stolen. After a lengthy investigation, she located more than one thousand hand-copied pages of the missing file. As the first Valentino biographer to access these records, Zumaya based her book *Affairs Valentino* upon this discovery. The wealth of new information divulged in these court records inspired ground-breaking directions in her research, culminating in her creation of the most accurate and documented account of Valentino's business and personal affairs.

In this *Companion Guide*, Zumaya shares the documents which are most relevant to her work. She believes this lost and now found archive of court records to be vital in documenting her work and in the understanding of her new and true story of silent film icon, Rudolph Valentino.

The S. George Ullman Memoir

In the days following the sudden death of Rudolph Valentino in 1926, his business manager and closest friend, George Ullman published a book titled, *Valentino As I Knew Him*. Before his own death in 1975, Ullman wrote a personal memoir about his life "behind-the-scenes" with Rudy. This memoir is a treasure trove of new anecdotes and information about the movie star's personal and business affairs. Lamentably, Ullman was, and still is, targeted by a few detractors who have aggressively misrepresented his story for decades. It was only after the recent discovery of Ullman's 1975 memoir, that an investigation was conducted into these allegations and documents uncovered which at last revealed the detailed truth about this iconic pioneer in celebrity management. This first publication of *The S. George Ullman Memoir* is accompanied by the entire transcript of Ullman's 1926, *Valentino As I Knew Him*.

Daydreams

When silent film icon Rudolph Valentino penned this book of poetry in 1923, he was waging a one man strike against his studio demanding higher quality production standards for his films. While he struggled to find a solution to this employment impasse, he delved into the occult and spiritualism and wrote his *Daydreams* poems. Shortly after Valentino's sudden death in 1926, his ex-wife, Natacha Rambova claimed her husband was adept at receiving messages from the astral plane via automatic writing. She also alleged that Valentino did not write the *Daydreams* poems, but instead transcribed them while in a trance, channeling them from his own spirit guides and deceased poets. The mystery of the true authorship of Valentino's fascinating "psychic" poems remains unsolved and continues to be the subject of discussion for Valentino's many ardent admirers.

The Infancy of the Myth by Aurelio Miccoli

Silent film star, Rudolph Valentino, spent the first nine years of his life in Castellaneta, a small city in southeastern Italy. This is the story of his Castellaneta years, a detailed, authoritative account of his essential familial, cultural, historical and even geographical influences. Author and native of Castellaneta, Aurelio Miccoli reveals "Rodolfo", as a curious yet difficult boy and daydreamer. His narrative is rich with the presence of the actual characters and places of Valentino's childhood days. With Miccoli's first hand familiarity with Castellaneta and his lifetime researching all available archives and locales, he has created a highly detailed, factual depiction of flora, fauna, streets and local history, all illustrated with full color photographs. *The Infancy of the Myth* is a scholarly study, an entertaining tale and a pictorial journey portraying the earliest events and influences of a little boy who became one of the world's most idolized screen icons.

In Italian:

L'Affare Valentino

La prima biografia in italiano di Rodolfo Valentino. Le Stelle e i Divi di Hollywood sono ben conosciuti anche per gli scandali che riescono a generare e la Stella del cinema muto Rodolfo Valentino non si discosta da questa tradizione. La Zumaya ha investito ben 15 anni in accurate ricerche sia sulla vita di Valentino sia all'interno della ristretta cerchia di chi gli era vicino, in modo particolare sul ruolo avuto dal suo caro amico ed amministatore-agente, George Ullman. L'innovativo lavoro svolto dalla Zumaya ridisegna drasticamente la storia di Valentino e rivela segreti esplosivi. Il lavoro della Zumaya è al 100% basato su fatti reali ed è supportato dalla scoperta di circa 400 pagine di documenti mai visti prima, relativi sia alla vita finanziaria sia alla vita personale di Valentino. Il fulcro di questo nuovo archivio è l'ancora non pubblicato diario di George Ullman, in cui egli racconta dei suoi rapporti con Valentino. L'archivio è completato da altri interessanti documenti, mai visti prima. Grazie a tutte queste nuove informazioni la Zumaya ha, finalmente, ricostruito il vero ritratto di Rodolfo Valentino ovvero dell'Uomo oltre al Mito.

L'Infanzia del Mito- Il Bambino Rodolfo Valentino

Il Mito del cinema muto Rodolfo Valentino, trascorse i primi nove anni della propria vita nella cittadina pugliese di Castellaneta. Qui si narra la storia dei suoi anni castellanetani; un dettagliato e autorevole racconto di quanto la sua famiglia, la cultura del periodo,

250

gli eventi storici e l'ambiente lo abbiano influenzato. L'autore di questo libro è un concittadino di Valentino essendo anche lui nato e cresciuto a Castellaneta, Aurelio Miccoli, e ci svela un "Rodolfo" bambino curioso anche se non semplice e un gran sognatore ad occhi aperti. Questo splendido e accurato racconto è arricchito dalla presenza di personaggi reali che hanno affollato l'infanzia di Valentino. Grazie alla sua familiarità con Castellaneta e la sua approfondita ricerca in tutti gli archivi locali disponibili, Aurelio Miccoli ha descritto un ambiente molto dettagliato riguardo alla storia locale, alle strade, alla fauna, la flora e la cultura dell'epoca; il tutto supportato da coloratissime immagini. "L'infanzia del Mito" è uno studio accademico, nonché un racconto divertente dei primi eventi e delle influenze su di un ragazzino che è diventato una delle icone dello schermo più idolatrate del mondo.

For more information please visit:

www.astralaffairsrambova.com

www.affairsvalentino.com

www.beyondvalentino.com

www.rudolphvalentino.org

Index

A

Acker, Jean, 7, 114, 215
Adelfia, 140
Adrian, 245
Affairs Valentino, 147, 241–42, 247–48
Affairs Valentino Companion Guide, 248
Affare Valentino, 250
Agni Yogi Forum, 149
Alberto Production Company, 144
Alex Rotov Scrapbook, 244
Alfred Marion Harned, 128
Alice Bailey's Arcane School, 119
Allen, Dawn, 123–25, 127, 129, 134
Alpha Gabriel, 15–16
Altai region, 120
American Opera, 124, 219
American Opera Company, 149
American Society for Psychical Research, 21, 30, 133
Anatole France, 241
Aphrodite, 245
Arcane School, 119, 122, 135
Argosy, 134
Arriba España, 247
Aum European Studios, 142, 150
Aunt Elsie DeWolfe, 27, 41, 169
Aunt Teresa, 4–5, 12, 34, 38–40, 42, 44, 46, 48–49, 51–52, 70, 72, 126, 135, 221
Aurelius Smit series, 33
Avella, 139
Avenue Kleber, 40
Aviation magazine, 15

B

Bailey, Alice, 119–20, 122, 126, 135, 181
Bamberger, Harry, 14–15, 30
Bamberger Circle, 14
Bamberger Circle of Saturday Nighters, 32
Bangalore, 134–35
Barbara Naomi Cohen-Stratyner, 149
Bari, 138
Barnum, 234
Bathesheba, 126
Beating Heart flowers, 89
Beecher, Janet, 30
Bernarr MacFadden, 9, 115–17
Bernhardt, Sarah, 103
Bess Houdini, 114
Billy Rose Theater Division, 244
Bimbo, 199
Black Feather, 8, 51, 73–74, 85
Black Pirate, 58
Blavatsky, 31–32, 95, 115, 120
   Helena, 32, 36, 40, 117, 119
Blavatsky's Secret Doctrine, 33
Boheme Film Company and partner, 139
Bollingen Foundation, 131
Bologna, 138
Bologna Archive, 244
Bombay Talkies, 134
Bonstelle, Jessie, 28
Bothmer, 241
Boutin/TASS, Dominique, 239
Broenniman, Edgar, 243
Broenniman, Eleanor, 1, 2, 34, 36
Brown, Cora, 44
Brownell, John C., 13
Brown-Potter, Cora, 94
Bruneri, court ruling, 141

Burbank, Luther, 95
Burroughs, John, 96, 106–7

C
Camille, 6, 245
Campbell, William, 147
Campbell's Funeral Church, 56
CaNaTacha, 130
Canella, 141
Canneto, 138, 140
Cantonese Theater, 128
Cantor, Eddie, 29
Captain Kangaroo, 128
Carnegie Hall, 128
Carter, Howard, 130
Caruso, 69, 79, 81
  Enrico, 30, 117, 182
Cassio, 137–44, 150, 205, 209–10,
  246
Cassio Film Company, 139
Castellaneta, 139–40, 246, 249–
  51
Castellani, Carla, 142
Castle, Vernon, 90, 148
Caterina Avella, 139, 206, 209
Chakras, 132
Champs Elysees Theater, 219
Chaney, Lon, 127
Chaplin, Charlie, 99
Chateau Juan-les-Pins, 221
Chicago Historical Society, 244
Chicago Tribune, 149–50, 243
Cine Comoedia, 143
Classical Chinese Theater, 128
Claude Falls Wright, 1–3, 36,
  153, 243
Clive Brook, 14–15, 18, 20, 114,
  164, 166
Clustine, Ivan, 120
Cohen, Harry J., 13
Colorado state flag, 128
composographs, 116–17
Cora Brown Potter, 44, 173

Cosmic Circuit, 132
Curious Life, 124, 127, 147–49,
  230, 242
Curley Stecker, 148

D
Dame Partington, 234
Daniel Carson Goodman, 13
Daydreams, 9, 249
Dayton Daily News, 149–50
DeMille, Cecil B., 7
deRosa, 139, 141
Devika Rani Chaudhuri, 134
Devils Guard, 123
DeWolfe, Edgar, 27
Diana, 231
Dobbin-Bennett, Tasha, 241
Doll's House, 245
Domenico Cassio Guglielmi,
  139
Domenico Nicassio, 138–39, 143
Donna Shinn Russell, 18, 125
Dorothy Benjamin Caruso, 30
Dudley, William, 242

E
Egyptology, 131–32
Elizabeth Barret Browning, 9
Ella Wheeler Wilcox, 99
Epstein, Miriam, 15–16
Exhibitor's Herald, 137, 147, 150
Extraordinary Test, 26, 50

F
Fate Magazine, 200, 240, 243
Fifth Avenue, 118, 214
Figaro, 45
Filippo Lippi, 43
Film Booking Offices of
  America, 13
Film Daily Yearbook, 239

First World War, 28
Fitch, Clyde, 101–3, 148
Fontainbleau, 41
Forbidden Fruit, 245
Forrest, Arthur, 94
Foster Bailey, 135
Foxlair, 49
Franke Harling, 124
Frederick James Smith, 117, 149
French Riviera, 3, 21, 39, 44, 173, 239
Frohman, Charles, 101, 103, 104, 148

G
Gallica Archive, 148–49
Garrick Theater, 28
George Benjamin Wehner, 25, 157, 244
George Ullman Memoir, 147, 242, 248–49
Gladwell, Robert, 240, 243
Glanville, 131
Gobelin tapestries, 43
Goodman, Daniel, 13
Gottinger Miszellen, 241
Grant, Leslie, 33–34, 244
Graybar building, 119
Green Brothers Novelty Band, 29
Griffin, Russell, 166
Guglielmi, Alberto, 144

H
Hampshire Society for Psychical Research, 19
Hansen, Donald P., 240
Hardy, Sam, 166
Harned, Alfred, 246
Harned, Bob, 246
Harned, Robert L., 147, 149, 239, 241, 246

Hartford Theater, 147
Haslett, Annie, 26
Haslett-Wehner, George, 128
Hasselriis, 134
Hauver, Marian, 15
Hearst Press Syndicate, 133
Heights Opera Company, 128
Helena Petrovna Blavatsky, 30–31, 44, 63, 153, 176, 235
Herr, Ann, 148
Herron, Bobby, 148
Homeric, 39, 55–56
Hooded Falcon, 245
Hotel Majestic, 40
Hotel Saint Rafael, 122
Houdini, 19, 114
    Harry, 19, 114, 159
Howe, Herb, 147, 213
Hoyt, Harry, 20
Hoyt, Harry O., 14, 18, 114, 163
Hudnut, Richard, 21, 40, 42–43, 47, 124, 177, 221, 223
Hudnut, Winifred K., 148
Hudnut chateau, 43–44, 50, 54, 63, 175
Hudnut Gallery, 135
Hutchinson & Co, 242
Hyslop, George, 223

I
Imperial Russian Ballet, 27
Irving Kaufman, 29
Irving Schulman, 147, 150
Ivanovitch, Paul, 44–45, 121, 175–76, 239

J
Jacinta, 121
James Whitcomb Riley, 9
Jawaharlal Nehru, 134
Jenny, 9, 48, 51, 55, 71, 73–74, 226–29

Jesus, 231
Jovanović, Milan, 239
June Mathis, 48, 226–27

K
Kenyon, Doris, 99
Khyber Rifles, 134
King Tut Ankh Amon, 131
King Vittorio Emanuele III, 137
Kiss, Robert J., 138, 246
Klaw Theater, 121
Kosloff, 27–28
    Theodore, 28
Kullu Valley, 121, 124

L
Lagoon, Pearl, 1–2, 37
Laura Jean Libbey, 13
Leatherhead Court, 27, 41
Lederer, Greta, 128
Leighton, George, 128
Leslie Grant Scott, 33, 121–22,
    133, 243–44
Liveright, Horace, 242
Lloyd's Film Storage Facility,
    142
Lockwood, Harold, 97–100, 148
Loie Fuller, 173
London archivist, 138, 246
London Ballet, 27
Lord Byron, 9
Lucero Rabaudi, 246
Lucis Trust, 135

M
MacFadden, 9, 115–17, 147
Madam Valentino, 149, 241, 247
Madam Valentino Addendum,
    240–41, 247
Madam Valentino Archive, 147–
    48, 150

Mallen, 149, 240–41
    Frank, 116, 149
Mallorca, 129–30, 199
Manassa, Colleen, 241
Margreta Overbeck, 128
Mark Hasselriis, 119, 131–32, 134,
    147, 149
Master Building, 121, 125–26
Master Institute, 119, 121
McCutcheon, John L., 137
Mesolope, 8–9, 50, 74, 228
Messalina, 22, 214–15
Miccoli, Aurelio, 139, 246, 249,
    251
Michael Morris Madam
    Valentino Archive, 239
Michigan Conservatory of
    Music, 27–28
Monaco, 44
Monrovian Mission, 37
Monsieur Beaucaire, 10, 245
Monteleone Giovanni, 140, 142,
    144, 239, 246
Mordkin, Mikhail, 120
Morris, Michael, 147, 149–50,
    247
Morris & Zumaya, 149–50
Moviesound, 142
Moviesound device, 142
Mulladay, Albert, 15
Mundy, 123, 127, 134, 136
Murray, Mae, 129
Museum of Religion and
    Philosophy, 124, 126
Mystic Science Magazine, 221
Mythological Papyri, 131

N
NARA, 244
National Library of France, 239,
    244
New Milford, 132
New Movie Magazine, 147, 213

New York City Symphony
  Orchestra, 128
New York Daily News, 148, 150,
  244
New York Evening Graphic, 12,
  115, 182–84
New York Evening Graphic's
  Composographs, 115
New York Theosophical
  Society, 32–34, 119, 125
Nicaragua, 1, 3, 34, 37
Nightingale, Florence, 81
Nobel Peace Prize, 120
Norman Bel Geddes, 121
North Star, 80

O
Ochsenschlager, 240
Ojibwa Indian, 85

P
Palace Theater, 35, 64
Palma, 129
Paris Opera Ballet School, 27
Passion Play, 78
Paternoster Row, 117, 242
Pathé, 133
Pathé Company, 132
Pathé Manhattan Studios, 139
Pavlova, Anna, 120
Peerless Quartet, 29
Pelley, 127–28, 242
Perrone, Angelo, 241
Peter Paul Rubens, 43
Philadelphia Museum, 132
Phipps, Sally, 149, 246
Phoenix Art Museum, 132
Photoplay magazine, 117, 148–
  49
Physical Culture, 115
Pickford, Mary, 119
Picture Play Magazine, 243

Plotnikoff, Eugene, 128
Point Loma, 123
Pola Negri, 38–39, 99, 113–14, 116
  girlfriend, 56
Polyclinic Hospital, 45
Preobrajenska, Olga, 120
Prince Film Producing
  Company, 137, 139, 142,
  204
Princeton University Press, 241
Professsor Miccoli, 140
Providence, 143
Psychical Research, 19–21, 30,
  133
Puglia, 140, 143, 246
Purple Vial, 35, 121
PVG Publishing, 242

Q
Quirk, Jimmy, 99, 148

R
Rachel Del Gaudio, 246
Ramsesses VI, 131
Reachi, Manuel, 168
Reginald Thomas Maitland
  Scott, 33
Reid, Wallace, 148
Renault, Camille, 141, 150
Riverside Drive, 121, 125, 127, 196
Robert Browning, 9
Roerich, Helena, 119, 121–22,
  126, 194, 241
Roerich, Nicholas, 120, 122, 194
Roerich Master Building, 127,
  196
Roerich Museum, 124
Roerich Society, 119, 121–23, 126,
  138, 239
Rotov, Alex, 120, 127–28, 190,
  246
Rousseau, 43

Rudolph Valentino Intime, 54, 115

S
Saint Agnes, 245
Saint Cyr, 43
Sainted Devil, 245
Salomé maria 240, 245
Saturday Nighters, 14–15, 32–33
Schenck, Joe, 132
Schnitzer, 13
Scott, Leslie, 33, 134
Secret Doctrine, 31, 119
Ses Coves, 130
Shaughnessy, Michael, 25
Sheik, 7, 14, 29, 38, 41, 45, 108–9, 147
Sherlock Homes, 19
Silver Legion, 127
Sir Arthur Conan Doyle, 19, 33, 117, 231
Sir Oliver Lodge, 231–32
Snyder-Gray murder trial, 118
Spanish Civil War, 130
Spiral Nebulae, 235
State Pushkin Museum, 135
Stepno, Bob, 149
Strauss, Ernst, 15
Svengali, 22
Svetoslav Roerich, 122, 125, 134–35, 138, 194, 197
Swan, Emma, 241
Swanson, Gloria, 58, 119

T
Talbot Mundy, 123–25, 127, 130, 134, 136, 149, 192–93, 230, 236, 242
tarot cards, 19
Tataguni, 134
Taves Brian, 149, 242
Theater Champs Elyseés, 124

Theosophical Society, 31, 138, 239, 243
Thomas, Olive, 98, 100, 148
Thomas Wilfred Clavilux, 119
Tixier, 25
Tosca, 142
Train Bleu, 42
Tropic Madness, 143–44
True Mystic Magazine, 133
True Mystic Science Magazine, 148, 201, 240, 243
Turin, 241–42

U
Ullman, George, 4–5, 9–13, 45, 51, 55, 72, 119, 132–33, 135, 147, 221, 248, 250
Uncle Dickie, 43–47, 49, 51–52, 55, 65, 70, 85, 94, 121–22
United Artists, 5, 10
United States Federal Census, 244
Ursaiz de, 129, 199
Utah Museum, 132, 135, 150

V
Valentino As I Knew Him, 248–49
Valentino Death Prophecy, 221
Vassar, 242
Versailles, 27, 41
Vesuvio, 213
Viale Industria Pubblicazioni, 42, 241–42, 246
Villa Margueritas, 44
Villa Trianon, 27, 41, 169
Vita Gaetana Cesarea Guglielmi, 138, 140

W
Watts, Henry, 75, 77, 82, 85–86,

100, 108
Wawashang, 2
Wawashang River, 1, 3
Wehner, Herman, 26
Werner, Teresa, 135
White Cloud, 16–17, 21, 26, 30,
    32, 34, 40, 85–87, 128
William Dudley Pelley, 127, 242
Wollen, Ann, 149–50
Woman God Forgot, 245
Wright, Claude, 1–3, 34

Y
Yale University, 132, 240–41
Young Rajah, 245

Z
Zarbo, 224
Zumaya, Evelyn, 147, 242, 247
    48

Notes